FAMILY BUSINESS
SUCCESS STORIES

HOW AUSTRALIA'S ICONIC FAMILY
BRANDS HAVE STOOD THE TEST OF TIME

GRAEME LOFTS

Graeme Lofts' book offers a rich and insightful analysis of what makes a business thrive over time. The stories behind Australia's most celebrated family brands highlight the secrets of success not only in business but in life itself – a long-term vision, a positive spirit, the ability to reinvent and adapt, and the courage to persevere in the face of adversity.

Peter Fritz AM, Group Managing Director, TCG

Family Business Success Stories is about true grit. It provides thought-provoking insights into the resilience of eight family firms that have survived and thrived for over 100 years. Central to their success is the pivotal role the family plays in overcoming challenges and adapting to change, illustrating that family and business can be a powerful combination when planned for and managed effectively.

Associate Professor Chris Graves, Co-Founder and Director, Family Business Education and Research Group (FBERG), The University of Adelaide

Family firms are the engine room of the economy, but their embodiment of values such as trust and loyalty are of even greater value to society. Whether you already run your own business or are thinking of starting one, this book offers a wealth of wisdom about how to incorporate family business values into your venture.

Catherine Fritz-Kalish, Co-Founder of Global Access Partners

First published in 2019 by Major Street Publishing Pty Ltd
PO Box 106, Highett, Vic. 3190 E: info@majorstreet.com.au
W: majorstreet.com.au M: +61 421 707 983

Quantity sales. Special discounts are available on quantity purchases by corporations, associations and others. For details, contact Lesley Williams using the contact details above.

Individual sales. Major Street publications are available through most bookstores. They can also be ordered directly from Major Street's online bookstore at www.majorstreet.com.au.

Orders for university textbook/course adoption use. For orders of this nature, please contact Lesley Williams using the contact details above.

The moral rights of the author have been asserted.

 A catalogue record for this book is available from the National Library of Australia

ISBN: 978-0-6484795-7-4

Cover design by Simone Geary
Internal design by Production Works
Printed in Australia by Ovato, an Accredited ISO AS/NZS 14001:2004
Environmental Management System Printer.

10 9 8 7 6 5 4 3 2 1

Acknowledgements

This book could not have been published without the kind assistance of the eight family businesses who provided me with access to their archives and publications. I would like to thank the family members, employees and former employees of the eight families who generously gave their valuable time to tell their stories and assist me in researching the history of their businesses.

In particular, I would like to thank Steve, Ted, Bill, Hale and Peter Samson along with Jacqueline Wisdom, Tom Wisdom, Elisabeth Marris, Jill Anderson and Annie Horne of the Samson family; Dr Tim Cooper AM, Louise Cooper and Leanne Gelly of Coopers Brewery; Adam Furphy of J. Furphy & Sons; Sam Furphy of Furphy's Foundry; John Forsyth AM, Ann Verschuer and retired employee John Millard of Dymocks; John Graham AO, Ross and Caroline Brown of the Brown Family Wine Group; Garry, Allyn and Rachel Beard, along with Gillian Wise, of A.H. Beard; Russell Sloan and James Downey of Bulla Dairy Foods; and Simon Haigh, Pam McAllister and Julie Waltz of Haigh's Chocolates.

I'm indebted to Associate Professor Chris Graves, co-founder and director of the Family Business Education and Research Group (FBERG) at the University of Adelaide Business School and PhD candidate Michael Browne (whose area of research is family business), who provided assistance in locating resources, introduced me to some of the families and critically reviewed the manuscript.

I would especially like to thank my publisher Major Street Publishing – a family business – and its managing director Lesley Williams for having the faith in me to complete this project, sharing my enthusiasm for the stories and providing invaluable support, and London-based editor Pauline Phillips, who did a wonderful job of fine-tuning the manuscript. I am also grateful for the keen support and suggestions of my son Aaron Lofts.

Above all, I thank my wife Dianne Lofts for her encouragement and patience throughout the two-year journey that led to the publication of *Family Business Success Stories*. Without her support and understanding I could not possibly have completed this book.

Contents

Foreword

Family Business Success Stories is a fascinating collection of stories from some of Australia's most iconic brands.

There are more than 1.4 million Australian family businesses operating in Australia – many of them highly successful. This book tells the stories of eight family businesses that have stood the test of time, operating for more than 100 years. They started out small and evolved to adapt to changes in society, technology and the marketplace before becoming the household names they are today. It was certainly not all smooth sailing either, as these businesses weathered recessions, wars and personal tragedies.

What strikes me about these family businesses is that their commitment to their work is matched by their devotion to each other.

In one particularly poignant moment, John Graham Brown talks about the wonderful lesson delivered to him by his father John Charles Brown of the Brown Family Wine Group. He spoke about his four boys having the opportunity to make something of the business. Using a vine cutting in his hand he broke it in half, saying, 'See how easily it's broken when there is only one?' He put the pieces together saying, 'See how much harder they are to break when there are two?' He put the four pieces together and said, 'Now it's almost impossible to break them. This is the strength you and your brothers can have if you work together.'

This really personifies the beauty of family businesses and their willingness to come together for a common goal. You'll see many examples of this throughout the book.

Another common theme is resilience. Each of the family businesses had to adapt to change and economic downturns and that is key to their success.

A great example of this was Alfred Haigh's leadership of Haigh's Chocolates during the Great Depression, which hit Adelaide severely as the unemployment rate soared. With consumers too poor to splurge on chocolates, Alfred decided to cut back on making his luxurious and more expensive chocolates and instead ramped up production of his cheaper confectionery, such as his penny chocolate frogs. He resisted the trend to reduce staff and instead expanded his retail network by supplying cafés and retailers in South Australia. This was an incredibly savvy move that helped Haigh's stay afloat during the world's worst economic crisis.

This is just one of many examples highlighted in the book that demonstrates the kind of agile adaptation that has contributed to the long-term viability of these family businesses.

Family Business Success Stories not only offers a unique insight into what life was like for Australians in the 1800s and 1900s, and the adversities they faced, but it also provides a number of valuable lessons that can be applied to businesses today.

One of the biggest lessons is that money isn't the be-all-and-end-all for these family businesses. For Coopers, which famously fought off a hostile takeover by Lion Nathan in the mid-2000s, family came first. On reflection of that chapter in Coopers' history, the family believes it survived because it had a good legal defence and, crucially, because most of the shares were in the hands of the fourth generation, who did not see a need to sell. At the time, Bill Cooper stood to make millions by selling his shares, but the desire to keep the family business was greater.

'I'm Bill Cooper of Coopers Brewery. If I sell my shares I get $60 million. Who do I then become? Bill Cooper, owner of condominiums. What does that mean?'

Coopers is now the largest family-owned brewery in Australia and it continues to be widely known for valuing its community, family members and employees. These values have been exemplified by many of the family businesses featured in this book, which is what makes these stories so engaging.

In summary, it has been a privilege to be a part of *Family Business Success Stories*. As a previous business owner and active advocate of Australian small and family businesses, I have found this book to be informative and enjoyable to read. Family businesses are inspiring in the way they approach business and the strategies they have used to keep them in the game and drive them forward. The stories in this book reflect true Australian spirit, innovation and eagerness to "have a go". To the families who shared their journeys – both the triumphs and failures – thank you. It's these business operators who prove every day that they are the engine room of our economy. Running a business is a challenge – especially if some of your employees are family members – but I admire the positivity, the passion and the relentless work ethic of these families.

Congratulations to author, Graeme Lofts, who has taken great care in capturing the hopes and dreams of the founders, the colourful characters, humour, setbacks and tragedies along the way.

Family Business Success Stories is a must-read for anyone interested in the business community. It sends a strong message to Australians about the social, cultural and economic contribution made by family-owned businesses.

Kate Carnell AO
Australian Small Business and
Family Enterprise Ombudsman

Preface

Approximately 70% of all Australian businesses are family owned. Together, they employ more than 50% of the Australian workforce. Australian family businesses represent a wide range of industries and skill sets including agriculture, manufacturing, mining, construction, retailing and food production. They are vital to Australia's economy – often the lifeblood of communities – and they operate throughout the country in capital cities, regional centres, small rural towns and the outback.

Family Business Success Stories traces the journeys of eight Australian family businesses that have been operating continuously in family hands for more than 100 years. In the pages of this book I describe how each business began and reveal the hopes and dreams of the founders, the colourful characters, the setbacks and the tragedies. The stories encapsulate the initiative, passion, entrepreneurship and resilience of the founders and the challenges faced by the generations that followed. Each of the featured family businesses began in humble circumstances – in a kitchen, shed, shop or backyard. Today, they span a total of 39 generations and employ more than 5,300 people.

The stories in the book are set against a backdrop of the history of Australia since 1829, when free settler Lionel Samson arrived at Fremantle in the fledgling colony of Western Australia. Samson's business, which is now the Lionel Samson Sadleirs Group, has manoeuvered itself through the Kalgoorlie gold rush, the depression of the 1890s, Federation and mining slumps. All of the businesses have faced two World Wars, the Great Depression of the 1930s, several recessions, a technology revolution, the Global Financial Crisis and ongoing worldwide economic instability. Some of them have withstood devastating family tragedies and been affected by natural catastrophes including floods and droughts.

While each of the businesses has survived for more than 100 years, some have faltered along the way but have picked themselves up, sometimes miraculously, and continued on their journey with even greater strength and resolve. How they have done this makes the stories even more fascinating – perhaps even stranger than fiction.

My interest in family businesses was kindled while I was undertaking research for my book *Heart & Soul: Australia's First Families of Wine* (John Wiley & Sons Australia, 2010). That book told the stories of the 12 inaugural members of Australia's First Families of Wine, who came together in 2009 to raise the profile of Australian family-owned wineries by showcasing the history, diversity and quality of the premium wine produced by the 12 families. I became intrigued by the passion of successive generations of the families and their ability to fight against adversity and bounce back from seemingly impossible challenges. Venturing beyond the wine industry was a natural next step.

Choosing which successful family businesses to include in the book was no easy task. I had to include businesses that not only had engaging stories, but which also provided lessons for others. They had to span at least three generations and reflect the diversity of Australian family businesses. That's when the enormity of the task of making the right choice became apparent.

Having made the arbitrary decision that they should have been established more than 100 years ago, I searched for family businesses that were enthusiastic about participating in the project and had:

- an engaging story

- a breadth of experience that would provide important lessons for other family businesses

- engagement with the community
- family involvement in industry bodies
- a commitment to environmental sustainability and gender equity
- a determination to keep the business in family hands
- availability of family members for interviews
- adequate records of company history
- a national footprint.

The stories told in this book demonstrate that there is much more to family businesses than just making a living. Garry Beard, member of Family Business Australia's Council of Wisdom and chairman of A.H. Beard, Australia's oldest bedding manufacturer, delivers a strong message about the social, cultural and economic value of family-owned businesses:

> 'If you look back at Australia over the past 200 years, the growth of this country has been accelerated by the youth and enthusiasm of its young people and it's been built on family businesses. The Aussie "have a go" approach has been an inspiration for a lot of people. We are recognised throughout the world as people who want to have a go. Australian family businesses exemplify that.'

It is clear that families who own and operate businesses, regardless of size, can learn from each other. While this can be done informally, I suspect that the majority of small family businesses operate in isolation, learning lessons the hard way, by trial and error, when they could be learning from the experiences of others. In today's environment, with so much bureaucracy and so many compliance issues, such as taxation and occupational health and safety, small family businesses can't afford to work in isolation. Starting a family business was much simpler in the days of Lionel Samson, Thomas Cooper, John Furphy, William Dymock and other pioneers more than a century ago.

I believe that with greater communication between Australian family businesses, particularly in their early stages, the rate of successful transition to future generations will improve. Of the approximately 1.4 million family businesses in Australia, only 2,500 are members of Family Business Australia (FBA), the peak body representing the sector. Yet FBA provides access to training and resources to assist individuals in family businesses in creating and maintaining a successful family business, along with opportunities for networking and sharing knowledge and experiences with their peers.

I have dedicated the final chapter of the book to reflecting on what the eight family businesses, despite their diversity, have in common. Chapter 9, Knowledge is power, provides lessons about resilience, entrepreneurship, family values, transfer of leadership and more. While this is not the place to list common characteristics, there is one that stands out in my mind, and that is the ability of family members to learn from both the successes and failures of themselves and their predecessors.

I hope that all readers find the stories told in *Family Business Success Stories* interesting, engaging and entertaining. If you own a family business or other small enterprise, I hope it gives you inspiration to continue to keep your business in family hands. If you work in a family business, I hope that it gives you greater understanding of the challenges your employers face on a daily basis.

CHAPTER 1

LIONEL SAMSON SADLEIRS GROUP

NIL DESPERANDUM

Photo on the previous page shows members of Lionel Samson & Son outside the building destroyed by fire in 1895. The two boys in front of the group are W.H.J. (Jack) Samson and his older brother Lionel.

THE LIONEL SAMSON SADLEIRS GROUP is Australia's second oldest family-owned business, operating continuously since 1829. Established at Fremantle in the fledgling colony of Western Australia, it began with two brothers opening a store to sell goods and livestock that they had brought with them as free settlers from England. In a little less than two hundred years it has grown into an Australia-wide importing, exporting, logistics and winemaking business that has spanned three centuries and six generations of the Samson family.

Today, the Lionel Samson Sadleirs Group employs about 350 people across sites in Fremantle, Perth, Melbourne, Sydney, Brisbane, Adelaide and the Great Southern wine region on Western Australia's south coast. In order to remain viable as a family business in the face of massive changes in Australian society and technology, the family has had no choice but to radically reinvent its business, both structurally and in the services it provides.

Migration to the colonies

Lionel Samson and his younger brother William arrived in Fremantle, then known as the Swan River Colony, in August 1829 on the barque *Calista* after a five-month voyage from Portsmouth, England. Many of the new settlers were not impressed with Fremantle and rejoined the *Calista*, which went on to Hobart and Sydney. No provision was made for their arrival and they were landed on a desolate beach on a cold winter's day. The only shelter for themselves and their possessions was the tents and tarpaulins they brought with them.

Raised in London by a wealthy Jewish family, both Lionel and William had been members of the London Stock Exchange and were attracted by the investment potential of the colony. The brothers were determined to succeed in Fremantle and moved quickly to form a business partnership, L. & W. Samson, dealing

3

in the merchandise they had brought from England and importing other goods for sale or auction.

Exactly one month after the brothers' arrival, they purchased two lots of a Fremantle subdivision and set up their first store. Lionel was quick to make friends and seemed to know everyone in the colony – from the Governor to the humblest settlers. He became the first settler in the colony to obtain a liquor licence and the business flourished. As a successful and popular merchant, Lionel was offered the post of Government Auctioneer by the colonial Governor. He declined, and the post was offered (at Lionel's request) to his younger brother. William accepted the post in October 1829 and relinquished it to Lionel in 1835. The appointment was finally transferred to Lionel Samson & Son and was held by the firm until 1900.

In May 1830 the Lieutenant-Governor of the colony appointed Lionel Samson as postmaster at Fremantle, an unpaid

The front door and sign on the Samsons' Cliff Street building remains intact.

post which he held for almost two years. Lionel's generosity ultimately led to his early resignation. He was suffering financially as a result of lending money to cash-strapped settlers and providing bags, sealing wax and string free of charge, along with the odd serve of brandy for those waiting for the mail to be sorted.

During 1830 Lionel and William purchased buildings on two lots in Cliff Street, Fremantle. One of the buildings was a stone cottage, which served as their residence. They both lived there as bachelors until they each married in the early 1840s and purchased separate homes. The cottage, known for many years as the Samson Cottage, remains in family hands today as the Fanny Samson Cottage Museum. The brothers used the second building as a store and auction house.

Lionel and William faced some challenges in the 1830s, including limitations in the range of stock available from incoming vessels. The brothers had to travel as far as South Africa on at least two occasions on specially chartered ships to purchase goods, which included rice, dried fruits, butter, honey, meat, wine, gin, beer and building materials. Exporting sheep, cattle, horses and dried fish became an important part of the business.

The colony suffered a shortage of cash, which forced the Samsons and other merchants to enter into bartering arrangements with their customers. This problem was alleviated in 1837 with the establishment of the Bank of Western Australia. Both brothers were quick to become shareholders and Lionel was appointed to the board of directors.

Despite the shortage of cash, Lionel was able to purchase two more lots in Fremantle, where he built a second store and auction house. Two years later he purchased a vacant lot in Perth on which he built an impressive house, which included an auction room and later, a retail store. The Perth house, on the corner of Barrack Street and St Georges Terrace in the city centre, became Lionel's home, while William remained in the stone cottage to take charge of the Fremantle stores. George Fletcher Moore, in his *Diary of Ten Years Eventful Life of an Early Settler in Western Australia*, wrote:

> 'They gave a house-warming ball and supper on Wednesday night and invited 150 people. Almost everybody was there and dancing kept up till sunrise.'

With the business now in both Perth and Fremantle, the brothers had to cross the Swan River regularly, which they did by boat or riding their horses and crossing by ferry.

Family matters

The 1840s proved to be a decade of change for the brothers and their business. Lionel sailed to England in 1842 to marry his much younger cousin Fanny Levi. The couple spent several months in England before returning to Australia. Fanny would have found living in the colony extremely hard, but she got on with it without complaint and became a well-respected Fremantle identity in her own right. Lionel and Fanny resided in Perth, where their first child, Michael was born in 1844, followed by Caroline (1845), Adelaide (1847), Louis (1849), Elizabeth (1850) and William Frederick (1855). Only Michael and William Frederick would eventually join their father in the business.

William moved to Adelaide with his wife and three children in 1846 to pursue what he saw as better auctioneering opportunities. In the same year his partnership with Lionel was dissolved by mutual agreement. William remained in Adelaide until his death in 1880 at the age of 77.

Lionel continued running the business as a sole trader after William's departure. He closed the retail store in Perth in 1848 but continued to hold auctions there twice a month. He began scaling down his operations – moving almost all remaining interests to Fremantle – and returned with his family to Fanny's cottage, to which he added a second storey, for the remainder of his life.

The Perth property was eventually leased to the Weld Club, a gentlemen's club in the English tradition and domain of the city's political and industry establishment, until 1892 and finally sold by auction in 1895.

Lionel had become recognised as a skillful orator and was given the honour of welcoming new Governors. He was also in keen demand as a chairman of public meetings, so in December 1849 as a natural next step, Lionel accepted an appointment to fill a vacancy on the Legislative Council, the sole House of Parliament of Western Australia at the time. There were no elections for Parliament until 1867. Lionel Samson held his seat in the Legislative Council until 1856 and again from 1859 to 1868, when he resigned at the age of 69.

As a Member of Parliament and Chairman of the newly formed Western Australian Chamber of Commerce, Lionel had a reputation for fighting for the rights of colonists and the improvement of road and mail services. At the same time, he continued to successfully operate his business, with the loyal support of his employees and friends. The colony was still small and there was a strong sense of community in Fremantle, where settlers were always willing to help each other out.

In 1856, Lionel and Fanny sent their eldest son Michael, aged 11, to St Peter's College in Adelaide to complete his education as a boarder. On his return home to Fremantle in 1859 Michael became an assistant in his father's business. Two years later he joined the Public Service as a clerk before deciding to rejoin his father's business several years later. In 1867, Lionel initiated a partnership agreement with Michael and the business became Lionel Samson & Son.

Michael was passionate about opera and the theatre and was President of the Fremantle Lyric, Operatic and Dramatic Club, which had a reputation for pushing the boundaries of moral standards. Apparently, this was one of the factors that led to him falling out with his father. Whether Michael chose to travel to China to oversee the export of sandalwood from Fremantle in 1875 or was sent by Lionel is unknown. When Michael returned from China, he left the business to rejoin the Public Service as a customs officer. Lionel then persuaded his youngest son, William Frederick, to join the business. William's experience as an accountant with the National Bank proved to be of great benefit and he was formally admitted to Lionel Samson & Son as a partner in 1877.

A changing of the guard

When Lionel died in 1878 at the age of 79, the business was left to his wife Fanny and son William as Lionel Samson & Son, Government Auctioneers, Merchants, General Auctioneers, and

Ship, Insurance and General Commission Agents. He left his gold watch to William, £50 to daughter Caroline and an annuity to daughter Adelaide. Daughter Elizabeth was not left anything because she had married into an affluent family. Michael was not mentioned in his father's will. Fanny remained a strong presence in the business but left its day-to-day operation to William. She continued to live in the Cliff Street cottage until her death in 1888 at the age of 64.

William Frederick Samson married Katharine Scott, daughter of harbourmaster Captain Daniel Scott, in January 1881. They had three children: Lionel (1881), Frances Caroline (1883) and William Henry Jack (1885). Like his father, William was politically active. He became a member of the Fremantle Municipal Council in 1883 and served for 11 years, including a two-year term as Mayor of Fremantle.

The business gained strength during the 1880s as Lionel Samson & Son expanded to become the largest importer of beer and spirits into Australia. After his mother's death in 1888 William was left in sole control of the business. Fanny had been well respected in Fremantle and her funeral was attended by a large number of prominent citizens, friends and family. In 1891, William demolished the stone building next to Fanny's cottage and oversaw the erection of a much larger office and warehouse on the site to accommodate the growing stock and administration requirements. Four years later the building, together with all of its stock, was destroyed in a fire. Although Fanny's cottage was damaged, it was saved from destruction by the quick arrival of the fire brigade. Fortunately, much of the Samson's merchandise was located in a nearby leased store.

Lionel Samson & Son managed to escape the effects of the depression of the 1890s because it coincided with a gold rush in Western Australia. The largest discoveries were made in Coolgardie in 1892 and Kalgoorlie in 1893. The population of the colony of Western Australia surged from 49,782 to more than 180,000 by Federation in 1901. Lionel Samson & Son shared in the prosperity of Western Australia experiencing a substantial increase in sales, particularly by those travelling to the towns that quickly grew in the goldfields.

Champagne cheaper than water

During the Western Australian gold rush of the 1890s, Charles Heidsieck Champagne was sold through several agents including Lionel Samson & Son, with most of it going to Kalgoorlie. Charles Heidsieck himself was so impressed that he travelled from France to find out what all the fuss was about. It had nothing to do with celebrating the gold rush. It was because the pipeline from Perth to Kalgoorlie hadn't been completed and champagne was cheaper than water.

In 1897, due to William's failing health, Fanny's nephew Philip Campbell was appointed as the first person to hold the title of manager of the business. New offices, a warehouse and a cellar, replacing the building lost in the fire, were completed in 1898. The cellar was used for bottling wine and spirits, which were imported in bulk from Europe. It now houses an impressive wine collection and provides a wonderful venue for the Samson family's special occasions and corporate events. The two floors above it are currently leased to other businesses.

Michael returned from China to Fremantle after his father's death in 1878 as Inspector of Customs and played no further part in Lionel Samson & Son. He was very active in the Freemasons and local government. After he retired from Customs, and five years after William's death, Michael became the second Samson to be Mayor of Fremantle, serving from 1905 until he died in office just over two years later. None of Michael's three children or their descendants ever took part in the family business.

William Frederick Samson died suddenly at his home in Fremantle in March 1900 at the age of only 44 and because he left no will, his widow Katharine became sole owner of Lionel Samson & Son. In time, she took in her three children as partners: Lionel, Frances Caroline (Mrs Cook) and William Henry Jack (Jack). Of the three children, only Jack, also known as W.H.J., played an active role in the business.

As a former Mayor of Fremantle, William's early death rocked the Fremantle community as well as his family. He had been highly respected in the business community and beyond, holding prominent positions including Consular Representative for France at Fremantle and directorships of the West Australian Shipping Association, the Fremantle Building and Investment Company, the Sun Insurance Company and the Swan Soap and Candle Company.

Under manager Philip Campbell the company continued to thrive, with Katharine Samson maintaining a strong presence as matriarch of the family. 'Apparently Katharine used to give the bank manager a really hard time,' says Elisabeth Marris (Frances Cook's granddaughter from the fifth generation). Philip Campbell's death in 1902 precipitated a succession of new managers who were not direct descendants of Lionel Samson. The managers guided the firm through the difficult years of World War I and later through the Great Depression.

Depression and war

From the time of Lionel's arrival in Fremantle, the Samson business had been building up an extensive portfolio of property that served as 'insurance' during the Great Depression of the 1930s. Fortunately also, the mining towns of Kalgoorlie and Boulder were booming again, with gold becoming a valuable commodity in response to the global economic turmoil. Lionel Samson & Son played a vital role in providing supplies to the revitalised gold mining towns. None of the company's employees were laid off during the depression.

A helping hand

During the Great Depression Jack Samson and his wife Beatrice set up a soup kitchen in their home. Numerous unemployed men and their families had set up camp nearby and they were often seen lining up outside the house. Later, during World War II, Jack and Beatrice sent food parcels to the company's agents throughout the world, who showed their gratitude by promising that Lionel Samson & Son would never lose their agencies.

Following the depression, Lionel Samson & Son's Cliff Street neighbour, R.C. Sadleir, another family-owned company, was experiencing troublesome times. It was established by Ralph Sadleir, the son of Irish settlers, in 1895 as a Customs, Shipping and Forwarding Agent. The business was being choked by the Western Australian government's restrictions on road transport to maintain the monopoly of the Western Australian government railways. The problem was exacerbated by R.C. Sadleir's inability to compete with larger operators, a lack of capital and an outdated, informal approach to managing the business.

Ralph knew that he was reaching the end of his working life and, as Jack Samson's grandson Steve Samson explains:

'Ralph Sadleir conceded that he no longer had the energy to do what was required and thought that Lionel Samson & Son could add capital and bright minds to keep the business going.'

The two companies already had a strong relationship. Jack Samson and Ralph Sadleir's brother Harry were close friends. In 1936, Harry Sadleir and Jack Samson negotiated a restructure in which Lionel Samson & Son acquired 90% of the shares in R.C. Sadleir. The Sadleir family retained 5% of its shares and the remaining 5% were issued to Jack's son Frederic Lionel (Bill) Samson.

Bill Samson joined Sadleirs as a customs agent and Sadleirs continued to operate as it had before the restructure. Harry was appointed managing director of the restructured R.C. Sadleir Pty Ltd in 1939. Sadleirs continued to operate as a separate business until another restructure in 2012.

The outbreak of World War II in 1939 presented new challenges for the growing businesses. The young men of both the Samson and Sadleir families joined the armed forces along with many of the staff, leaving both businesses virtually "on hold". Both imported and locally produced stock, including liquor and fuel, were in short supply, but Sadleirs was protected from rationing as the transport of freight was designated as an essential service.

Following the end of World War II, the staff returning from military service were re-employed. Fourth generation brothers Derek and Tony Samson returned to help manage Samson & Son and oversee a massive post-war expansion. Bill Samson studied accounting when he returned from war service and soon returned to the business in a critical role at Sadleirs.

Second generation Sadleir brothers Paddy and Nix returned from the war in poor condition. Paddy was discharged in 1944 after contracting malaria in New Guinea and resumed his management position at Sadleirs. Nix had only worked in the family business during school holidays and took no further part in the business.

Post-war diversification

In response to the limited supply of traditional stock and the changing economic climate following World War II, Lionel Samson & Son purchased a controlling interest in Western Bottling Pty Ltd, bottlers and distributors of Coca-Cola products throughout Western Australia (which later became Coca-Cola Bottlers (Perth) Pty Ltd). That company later took over Golden West Aerated Water, bottlers of cordials and other soft drinks, as well as a number of dry-cleaning businesses. New warehouses, stores and offices in Fremantle were purchased to accommodate the expansion.

The firm also increased its exposure to the growing liquor industry by purchasing the Westral Wine and Spirit Agency and Westralian Hotels, which gave it direct ownership of several Perth and Fremantle hotels. It also acquired other liquor agencies and a controlling interest in Engineering Facilities Pty Ltd, which specialised in north west mining projects and steel fabrication.

In 1948, with the business expanding rapidly, Jack Samson decided to incorporate Lionel Samson & Son as a proprietary company and create three holding companies: Calista Pty Ltd, F.C. Cook & Co. Pty Ltd and W.H.J. Samson Pty Ltd. The three holding companies were set up to ensure that the interests of Jack's siblings, Lionel and Frances, were looked after, as well as his own. Jack, Lionel and Frances were the only remaining grandchildren of Lionel Samson still associated with the business. Calista was named after the barque on which Lionel and his brother William first sailed to Fremantle. F.C. Cook referred to Frances Caroline's married name and W.H.J. Samson referred to Jack.

Following the retirement of Derek Samson and non-family manager Roy Ward, Derek's younger brother Coulston Scott (Tony) was appointed as managing director of Lionel Samson & Son in 1952, a position he retained for almost 30 years. Tony was well respected in the liquor trade and played a prominent role in industry bodies.

Paddy Sadleir passed away in 1960 at the age of 46, six years after taking on the role of managing director following the death of his uncle Harry. Paddy was the last member of the Sadleir family to work in the business. The Samson family, along with the general manager of Sadleirs, Fred Leivers, were now in control of the transportation side of the business with Bill Samson in the role of chairman. Paddy's widow sold most of her husband's shares shortly after his death and the last of the Sadleir family's shares were sold to the Samson holding companies in the late 1980s.

During the 1960s, Sadleirs successfully moved into interstate haulage by road. The small and archaic Fremantle depot was hopelessly inadequate and even the larger depot purchased in 1958, in Newcastle Street just outside the Perth CBD, was at its limit. In the late 1960s, the company purchased a large site at Kewdale, which was serviced by rail as well as road. It opened a freight depot, complete with generous warehouse space, in 1970 while Sadleirs was still a relatively minor part of the entire business. By the mid-1970s, the diverse interests of what had become the Samson Group of Companies included liquor wholesaling, hotel and liquor store ownership, transport, laundry, engineering, investment and travel agencies.

The following decade, what was now the Lionel Samson Group of Companies began disposing of hotels and liquor stores and other less profitable interests to fund the development of its interstate road transport depots through R.C. Sadleir Pty Ltd, which was still being managed separately. Much of the long-held property in Fremantle was also sold.

Generation five

In 1982, Tony Samson retired and founder Lionel's great great grandson Bill Samson (not to be confused with Jack's son Frederic Lionel (Bill) Samson) took over the reins as managing director. At this time the Australian and international wine industries were experiencing major changes. Bill Samson says:

'As wine volumes grew, major Australian producers began to open their own offices across the states, including here in Perth.'

14

Wine and other liquor distribution was becoming more competitive and it became clear that a change of direction was needed for the Samson business, away from liquor and more focused on transport and other profitable services or products. The last bottle of spirits was produced on the Samson bottling line in December 1984.

When Bill Samson resigned to open his own business, he was succeeded as managing director by Geoffrey Scott Cook, another great great grandson of Lionel Samson. The expansion of the business continued, particularly in transport and freight. In 1991, the company purchased packaging company Paccom International, which remains today as part of the Lionel Samson Sadleirs Group. This acquisition proved to be astute as packaging fitted well into the existing transport and freight facilities.

> Plantagenet is one of the most trusted wine brands in Australia and continues to expand its varietal range and strive for excellence in winemaking.

In 1994, the Samson Group of Companies formed a joint venture with French-based Remy Australie. Named Lionel Samson (SA) Pty Ltd, the joint venture company sold, marketed and distributed Remy Australie wine and spirits in South Australia and the Northern Territory. The venture was a dismal failure and the company was wound up barely a year later.

Later in 1994, the Samson family began what was to become a three-stage acquisition of Plantagenet Wines with the purchase of a one-third share. A further one-third share was acquired one year later, giving the Samson Group a majority interest, and the remaining shares were purchased in 1999. Plantagenet Wines had its own proud heritage as one of the first vineyards and wineries of the Great Southern wine region on Western Australia's south coast. Plantagenet is one of the most trusted wine brands in Australia and continues to expand its varietal range and strive for excellence in winemaking.

The rise and rise of Sadleirs

By the turn of the 21st century it had become clear that the future of the family business depended on developing its transport and logistics assets. In March 2005, a new company was formed, called Storsack Paccom Pty Ltd; a joint venture with the Storsack GmbH Group, a global packaging manufacturer based in Germany. Sadleirs later took total ownership of the venture and it has since been rebranded as Sadleirs Packaging, based at Kewdale.

When it became apparent that the 40-year-old Kewdale terminal did not have the capacity to handle the increasing volume of freight, Sadleirs spent $20 million upgrading the offices and freight facilities. The upgrade was completed in 2009. Director Steve Samson, who played a major role in the design, expressed the hope that the new and spacious working environment would entice more family members into the business:

> 'The existing office facilities were pretty bad, and we couldn't get anyone to work there. We wanted to transform the terminal into something special and create a really good place to work.'

In 2012, Sadleirs and Lionel Samson & Son joined to become what is now known as the Lionel Samson Sadleirs Group (LSSG) in the biggest restructure of the business since incorporation in 1948. The aim of the restructure was to lock the Samson and Cook families, all descendants of Lionel Samson, into one family business. At the time, members of both families were spread across Sadleirs and Lionel Samson & Son.

The small boards that governed Samson & Son, Plantagenet and the Sadleirs transport, international and packaging companies were amalgamated to create a single governance board that is responsible for the operations of all component companies. This board is required to include a minimum of two family members and is answerable to a separate board, which oversees the three holding companies created in 1948. The latter comprises exclusively family members representing the three shareholder groups.

The Lionel Samson Sadleirs Group now consists of five companies:

1. Sadleirs Logistics, which operates throughout Australia, relies heavily on rail services and minimises the use of road transport, which reduces both costs and the company's carbon footprint.

2. Sadleirs Global, which operates globally, facilitating goods importation and exportation to and from Australia by partnering with other customs agencies throughout the world.

3. Sadleirs Road Distribution Services, which services the mining and energy industries in the north west of Western Australia where there are no rail services.

4. Sadleirs Packaging, which sources plastic goods from Asian manufacturers and sells to Australian and New Zealand companies.

5. Plantagenet Wines, which produces wines for the Australian market and currently exports to nine countries including the United Kingdom, USA, Canada and China.

Reflections

As the second oldest continuously operating family business in the country, the Lionel Samson Sadleirs Group is rightly proud of its heritage. The family motto, *Nil Desperandum* – in English, 'Do not despair' – reflects the resilience that has been central to the survival of the business since Lionel Samson established it in Fremantle in 1829. Since then, it has not only survived global conflicts, economic downturns and dramatic changes in its primary enterprise of importation and liquor distribution but completely reinvented itself to become a dynamic national and international logistics group of companies with a quality winery to top it off.

Reflecting on the success of the business, fifth generation shareholder Jacqueline Wisdom says, 'Whenever the business looks like sinking it comes back, even stronger than it was before.' But it's not just resilience. Other family members cite honesty, integrity, hard work, reinvestment in the business and diversification as factors in the longevity and success of the business. 'Lionel gave us a good moral compass,' says operating board member Ted Samson.

Steve Samson, fifth-generation shareholder, commented on the company's longevity while giving evidence to the Parliamentary Joint Committee on Family Businesses in Australia in 2012:

> 'To give you our story, during the very tough times during the 1970s and 80s, when things were very, very tough, we made sure that we never sacked any person who was an employee of our business, because that is what the family wanted to do. They were willing to forgo a dividend, a profit, to make sure that we supported and protected those employees.'

Steve Samson admits that there is an element of luck in the company's success:

> 'We did have shares in mining companies at the right time. We managed to buy a lot of hotels, which were going cheap. On the other hand, we've made our own luck. We were willing to diversify and try new things. We could have remained as a customs agency and we'd be out of business by now.'

There have been a number of people outside the Samson family who have made valuable contributions to the business. After second generation William's early death in 1900 with no will – and with no family members having the experience needed to run the company – a succession of external managers oversaw operations under the watchful eye of William's widow Katharine until she died in 1941 aged 95. The third of the non-family managers, Harry Price, worked for the Samson family for 53 years. From the end of World War II until the turn of the century, members of the Sadleir and Samson family managed the business, with support from several long-serving non-family members.

> Whenever the business looks like sinking it comes back, even stronger than it was before.

Of particular importance was Fred Leivers, who joined Sadleirs in 1924, aged 14, as an errand boy then managed the Fremantle office from 1938 and later became general manager until 1977. He remained on the board until 1990, having served the business for a remarkable 66 years. Another notable contributor was Des Lambert, who started as an office boy in 1937 and worked his way up to company accountant. He was an integral part of Samson for 47 years before retiring in 1984 and was also the company's unofficial historian.

Preserving the history of the business

Fanny Samson's cottage in Cliff Street, Fremantle, is still owned by the family business. To mark the 150th anniversary of Lionel Samson & Son and the state of Western Australia, the company converted the cottage's first floor into a museum, which houses a collection of historic documents and other company memorabilia. Below the museum is a theatrette, fitted with the original seats from Perth's historic His Majesty's Theatre. The museum opens for special events and the theatrette is used for shareholder meetings. The original cellar is used for private and family events. As the home of Lionel, Fanny and their six children until Fanny's death in 1888, Fanny Samson's cottage remains the spiritual centre of the Lionel Samson Sadleirs Group.

Fanny Samson's renovated cottage.

Moving forward

There is no doubt that the majority of the approximately 100 living descendants of Lionel Samson's son William want to keep and grow the business. As well as the obvious benefit to them of receiving dividends, the business has a long and proud history. The pride of family members in being the second oldest family-owned business in Australia – and, as some are keen to point out 'the oldest family-owned business on the mainland' – is, in itself, motivation to keep it in their hands.

The key to the future of the business as a family-owned enterprise is ensuring that future generations are actively involved in its management alongside non-family members who may be better qualified or more capable.

When second generation William became too ill to continue in 1897, managers were appointed from outside the family because the next generation wasn't ready to take over. A similar situation was emerging in 2011, while the business was in the process of reinventing itself as the Lionel Samson Sadleirs Group and very few family members worked in the business. The family was becoming distant from the business and it was moving towards being run by non-family members. The company saw this as a serious threat to the future of the business as a family-owned enterprise, and established a family council whose purpose was primarily to keep the growing family together and engaged in the business. With the support of Family Business Australia (FBA), through its professional development programs, the family council developed a charter to set out "rules of engagement" that would provide a formal framework for family interaction with the business and the three holding companies.

The family council acts as a conduit between all family members and the board of the three holding companies. It has no direct role in governance of the business. It ensures that family issues are discussed before they develop into a crisis that could damage the business. The council meets every second month.

Current CEO Ian Kent, who is not a member of the Samson family, believes that the family council is fulfilling its role. 'The business is well structured,' he says. 'Communication is the key and despite the large number of shareholders we do that well with the help of the family council.' He adds, 'I've worked with lots of family businesses but this one works. It's not easy to entrench family values when you are scattered all over the world.'

One of the subcommittees of the family council was the Samson Family History Group, which is dedicated to preserving the history of the business, buildings, records and artefacts for the family and the community. The Group, passionately led by Jacqueline Wisdom, is now an incorporated body, which meets regularly in the Cliff Street wine cellar.

Succession planning is critical to the ongoing success of the Lionel Samson Sadleirs Group. Although the business has experienced long and successful periods under the management of non-family members, there is clearly a desire to increase the participation of the family. Fifth generation Bill Samson says:

'Naturally we'd like to see family members managing the company but, for the sake of the future generations of shareholders, senior appointments must be made on merit.'

According to Bill's cousin Peter Samson, 'We should nurture the next generation. The last generation didn't really do it for us,' he says. Peter's brother Steve Samson agrees, 'The next generation is better qualified and more experienced than we were. We need to ensure that they are interested in working for the family business.'

Although few members of the sixth generation participate in the business at present, there is a sense of optimism that this number will increase with the growing awareness of the importance of succession planning and the additional interest generated by the work of the family council. Steve Samson's son Hale joined Sadleirs more than 13 years ago as a forklift driver and has worked his way up through the business to become the operations manager of Sadleirs Road Distribution Services. He has brought his technical expertise and experience to bear on the department to greatly improve its efficiency.

Another member of the sixth generation, Tom Wisdom, joined the business as a director in 2014 after working for the Commonwealth Bank as a senior analyst and director of specialised agribusiness solutions for nine years. He currently holds the roles of chief commercial officer of the Lionel Samson Sadleirs Group and general manager of Plantagenet Wines. When he joined the business, Tom admits feeling that his family was emotionally detached from the business and 'there was a certain malaise about involvement'.

The sixth generation is represented on the operating board by Bill Samson's son Angus as a non-executive director. Angus is a qualified chartered accountant and is currently tax manager for

Japan Australia LNG (MIMI) Pty Ltd, which has significant LNG interests in Western Australia.

Looking to the future, the company sees greenhouse gas emissions and climate change as major challenges. Since its move to Kewdale, Sadleirs Transport has used rail in preference to road transport wherever possible, which reduces costs and its carbon footprint. The use of electric or hybrid road transport is already being explored. Hale Samson believes that driverless trucks may be used in the remote north west of Western Australia, where driver fatigue is a serious safety issue.

The performance of the Lionel Samson Sadleirs Group and its predecessors has been relatively unpredictable, with economic fluctuations and government intervention in the liquor and transport industries. The boom–bust nature of the Western Australian economy has created both setbacks and new opportunities for the business since the discovery of gold in Kalgoorlie in 1893. The acquisition of Nexus Freight in 2010 to expand its services into north west Australia and the Northern Territory is an example of this. Only six years later it was sold to the Toll Group as it had become unprofitable. At the time of the acquisition, Western Australia was a major beneficiary of a mining boom that was at its strongest in its north west. Within four years the boom was over, and the group had to make the tough decision to sell. On the positive side, the sale provided the funding for a much-needed overhaul of the group's information technology systems, which provided long-term benefits for all company operations.

Because of its concentration in Western Australia, the success of the Lionel Samson Sadleir Group has always depended on its ability to respond quickly and strategically to rapid change.

> Looking to the future, the company sees greenhouse gas emissions and climate change as major challenges.

It has learned from its own history of management, achieving a balance between family and external management and of diversification, whether successful or not. Only months after the arrival of Lionel Samson in Fremantle more than 190 years ago, the family business began to acquire property assets, which have been sold in hard times or to take advantage of an opportunity. The business to this day continues to strategically acquire property, which Steve Samson describes as 'patient capital', to be developed or disposed of at some time in the future for the benefit of the next generations of Lionel Samson's descendants.

In 2029, the Lionel Samson Sadleir Group will celebrate its two hundredth anniversary. Its history suggests that it will remain in family hands for many years to come in a very different and constantly changing world.

CHAPTER 2

COOPERS LTD

BORN TO BREW

Photo on the previous page is the Coopers display at the South Australian Centennial Exhibition in the new Centennial Hall at the Wayville Showgrounds in 1936.

THE STORY OF COOPERS BREWERY began in a modest suburban Adelaide home where 35-year-old Thomas Cooper created his first batch of ale in 1862. Thomas had no knowledge of brewing and relied on an old family recipe brought from his birthplace in Yorkshire. He was so impressed with the taste of his ale that he began to share it with friends and neighbours. Having already tried his hand as a shoemaker, stonemason and dairy farmer, Thomas had accidentally stumbled upon his true destiny as a brewer.

More than 150 years later, Coopers Brewery is Australia's oldest and largest family-owned brewery, producing ales and stouts based on Thomas Cooper's original brewing recipe and methods, along with lagers and other beers brewed under licence, non-alcoholic beer, malt extracts and home-brew concentrates.

The beginning

Thomas Cooper, the youngest of 12 children, was born in Yorkshire in 1826. As a young adult Thomas, a devout Methodist, worked as a shoemaker. With the future for his business looking bleak, he set off for the new colony of Australia in May 1852 with his pregnant wife Ann and two infant children, William and Sarah Ann. Tragically, during the 86-day voyage Sarah Ann became ill and died.

With so many new arrivals in the fledgling colony of South Australia, Thomas had plenty of work as a shoemaker before learning a new trade as a stonemason, apparently for health reasons. By early 1856 he was able to buy a block of land in the suburb of Norwood and obtain a loan so that he could use his new skills to build a house. He rented additional land, purchased some cows and established a small milk delivery service.

Six years later, Thomas' first ale was brewed as a tonic for his ailing wife Ann, using a recipe that she had brought from Yorkshire. Once sampled by his friends and neighbours, there were requests for more and word of his new flavoursome beer spread quickly through the growing settlement of Adelaide. It occurred to Thomas that he could supplement his income by brewing more batches of ale from the same recipe, selling it in second-hand bottles of various shapes and sizes as well as in 5-gallon kegs.

By the end of 1862 Thomas had mortgaged his home to build a brewhouse on his own land, fit it with new equipment and extend his existing cellar so that he could increase production. He sold his milk run and all but one of his cows, committing himself totally to his future as a brewer. Thomas experimented by varying the proportions of malt, hops and water in the mix and making minor changes to the brewing process. The quality of his ales varied, and he sold those that he felt were inferior at lower prices. By 1868, despite reasonable sales of his beer, Thomas was in financial stress due to debt and the costs of raw materials for brewing. At the same time, his family was still growing, with four sons and three daughters to care for and educate.

Towards the end of 1869 Thomas could not meet his mortgage obligations and his creditor took possession of his property, including land, buildings and brewing equipment. He had clearly over-committed himself but narrowly escaped bankruptcy.

Thomas moved his family to a rental property in the nearby suburb of Kensington and borrowed from his life insurance policy to set up a small brewing plant that allowed him to produce enough ale to supply his regular private customers in 1870 and 1871. He was determined to give his children the best possible start in life and managed to pay for the girls' tuition and keep three of his sons at the prestigious Prince Alfred College, with some help from scholarships.

Thomas was dealt a cruel blow in July 1872 when his wife Ann died suddenly at the age of only 44 from what appeared to be a brain haemorrhage. He had already experienced far more than his fair share of family tragedy. Ann had borne Thomas five sons and six daughters, but only two of those six daughters survived infancy. The fact that he was able to keep his business afloat with his financial overcommitment and the ongoing barrage of family tragedy was a testament to his perseverance and resilience.

In the early to mid-1870s Thomas obtained small loans from benefactors who were confident of his ability to weather the storm so that he could continue to supply his regular customers. During this period, he resorted to his former trade of shoemaking to provide some much-needed additional income. Three of his sons were also working and contributed to the running of the household.

A man of faith

It might seem strange to some that Thomas Cooper, a devout Methodist, would become a brewer. However, although many of that faith were supporters of the temperance movement, its founder John Wesley encouraged the use of hops in the brewing of beer but was critical of spirits. Thomas was supremely confident that his brewing of beer was not a breach of his faith. He was a lay preacher of the Wesleyan Methodist Church and he travelled throughout the eastern suburbs of Adelaide to deliver sermons several times a month.

In July 1874 Thomas, at the age of 47, married Sarah Perry, who was 14 years his junior. Sarah cared for his younger children and by 1882 had given birth to seven sons and one daughter. Tragically, three of the sons did not survive infancy. The growth of this "second family" of Thomas was to have a major effect on the future structure of the business.

During 1877 and 1878, Thomas' accumulated experience and experimentation with brewing techniques began to pay dividends. The quality and output of his brews improved, and Thomas began repaying his debts and making small improvements to his brewery. His 21-year-old son John, who had been working as a librarian, joined Thomas in the business in 1878 and quickly established himself as an influential force in the brewery. The improvement in quality, output and sales accelerated and the business was able to invest in more advanced machinery to increase its output.

Because of his religious beliefs Thomas refused to supply public houses. He believed that beer should be consumed in the home and that the hotels were contributing to the plight of ordinary working men, who were spending more than they should on beer at the expense of their families. His brewery was one of the smallest of the 25 in the colony of South Australia in 1881. Thomas still only sold to private customers and delivered his beer by horse and cart. He had built up a largely affluent client base, whose loyalty had helped him through the difficult years.

In early 1881, Thomas purchased land in Statenborough Street, Upper Kensington (now known as Leabrook), took on even more debt and built a new, larger brewery that was to become the home of Coopers Brewery for 120 years. The first ale was brewed within months, and advertisements claimed that Coopers ale and stout was superior to all others. By the mid-1880s, production and sales had tripled.

The merging of other brewers to form larger and more efficient businesses, along with the depression of the 1890s, could have crushed the relatively small Coopers Brewery. However, three factors ensured its survival:

1. The temperance movement forced the closure of hotels on Sundays. The other brewers were almost entirely reliant on bulk sales to hotels but Coopers was not affected.

2. Its products were of a superior quality, which was ensured by the experience and knowledge of Thomas and John, and the contributions of four other family members in the brewery.

3. It had loyal and relatively affluent private customers.

*The brewery and Thomas Cooper's house in Upper Kensington (now Leabrook)
c. 1893. The telegraph pole on the left is ready for the connection of the telephone.*

Thomas died in 1897 at the age of 71. Although retired from daily involvement in the brewery for several years, he had continued to oversee the business. Thomas left all of his property and the business to the four eldest of his surviving sons: John, Christopher and Samuel from his first marriage, and Stanley from his second. He left instructions that his 15-year-old youngest son Walter should receive an interest in the business at the age of 25. His other sons and daughters were bequeathed cash or furniture and provision was made for his widow to be maintained in the family home. As it turned out, Walter moved to the Northern Territory to hunt buffalo before reaching the age of 25 and died of malaria at 26. The four brothers shared the responsibility of running the brewery but John was the guiding influence.

A new century; a new direction

The new partnership, now known as Cooper & Sons, made the decision to supply hotels, accepting that they could not expand the business while selling exclusively to private customers. Founder Thomas Cooper would almost certainly have disapproved of this decision, even though it was necessary to grow the business. By 1918 hotels accounted for 76% of sales despite the introduction of mandatory 6pm closing of hotels in 1916.

The success of sales to hotels led to the expansion of the brewery with the purchase of adjoining land and new buildings. John, Stanley and Samuel Cooper also purchased nearby allotments privately, providing a convenient buffer between the brewery and its neighbouring residents. The other partner, Christopher, passed away before the expansion and was eventually replaced as a partner by John's son Frank in 1918.

Cooper & Sons increased its production during the two decades of the new century by almost 500% due to both the introduction of its ale and stout to hotels and its reputation for high quality. In 1923, with the oldest partner John aged 66, the growing size and value of the business, and the inevitable entry of more members of the third generation into the business, a restructure became necessary. It made sense to cease the partnership arrangement and Cooper & Sons was incorporated as a limited liability company to facilitate the involvement of other Coopers in the company. Just over 80% of the shares were distributed equally between John and Stanley, with about 18% going to the estate of the late Samuel's deceased widow. John's son Frank and Samuel's son Wilfred were each issued a token share.

To ensure ongoing participation of both sides of founder Thomas' family in the management of the company, the shares were designated as "A" and "B". "A" shares were issued to descendants of Thomas and his first wife Ann. "B" shares were issued to descendants of Thomas and his second wife Sarah. Directors were to be appointed equally by "A" and "B" shareholders, making John an "A" director and Stanley a "B" director.

Demand for Coopers ale and stout, particularly the latter, increased significantly in the 1920s, and the company and its directors prospered. Despite continuing expansion of the brewery, it took until 1928 before the company was able to match the demand with production.

During the Great Depression of the 1930s, beer consumption in South Australia fell by 50% and Cooper & Sons suffered equally with its larger competitors. Beer had become a luxury item for most families who were struggling to keep their children fed and make ends meet. To make matters worse, following pressure from other brewers and the hoteliers, Coopers had agreed in 1929 to cease selling to private customers, which left it totally reliant on sales to hotels.

Rather than force its employees into the ranks of the unemployed, Coopers retained them on a part-time basis, keeping the brewery running by having them work alternate weeks. Expenditure on plant maintenance was kept to a minimum and shareholder benefits were reduced, as were bonuses and gifts to family and long-serving employees.

In the years following the depression an attempt to abandon 6pm closing in hotels was frustrated by the temperance movement, limiting the expected increase in beer consumption. Wage growth, an increase in the cost of malted barley and a rise in excise duty limited sales and profits. Coopers responded by boosting its efforts to sell interstate, but this had little impact because consumers were fiercely loyal to the beers brewed in their own states.

> Rather than force its employees into the ranks of the unemployed, Coopers retained them on a part-time basis, keeping the brewery running by having them work alternate weeks.

The first change to the board of directors since incorporation was forced by the death of John Cooper at the age of 78 in July 1935. John was highly respected throughout the South Australian brewing industry, having served as chairman of the South Australian Brewers' Association for more than 10 years.

He was recognised as a fair, caring and astute man and had earned the loyalty and affection of all who worked at Coopers as the "man in charge" for almost 40 years. After his funeral, the employees of Cooper & Sons marched down Statenborough Street behind the hearse.

John's son Frank took his father's place as an "A" director; his half-brother Stanley, a "B" director, became chairman. Two new directors, John's son Andrew and Stanley's son Tom, were appointed to represent the "A" shareholders and "B" shareholders respectively. John left all his shares to his sons and daughters.

Treading water

In October 1938 Stanley, the last of the second-generation directors, died of typhoid, leaving the board totally in the hands of Thomas Cooper's grandsons. Frank assumed the role of chairman and Stanley's son Ray was appointed a "B" director. Within a year Cooper & Sons was the only remaining privately owned brewery in South Australia. Beer sales were dominated by the South Australian Brewing Co. (SAB) and although Coopers accounted for less than 10% of the state's beer sales, it boasted 70% of the stout market.

The outbreak of World War II brought numerous problems to the brewery. Director Ray, Frank's son Geoff, a fourth-generation Cooper who had joined the family business, and a substantial number of other employees, enlisted in the armed forces. Ray served in the Middle East, the Western Desert and New Guinea, reaching the rank of Captain. Geoff served in England and was awarded an MBE before fighting in Alexandria, Tobruk and New Guinea, where he was seriously wounded. Back home, Cooper & Sons sponsored community concerts to raise money for the Fighting Forces Comfort Fund. The concerts, usually held in town halls, were broadcast live on Adelaide radio station 5AD.

The impact of the war on Cooper & Sons worsened as it progressed. As well as labour shortages, materials became hard to obtain and a new payroll tax was introduced in 1942. A cut of one-third of all beer production was ordered by the Federal Government to conserve grain and, apparently, to discourage spending on alcohol, leaving people with more to spend on buying bonds called "Victory Loans" to help fund the war effort.

The shortage of labour led to women being employed at the brewery for the first time. The first two women employees were family members – fortunately, because there were no toilet facilities for females in what had been an all-male workplace, so they had to go next door to Tom's house when nature called. It wasn't until the 1960s that women were employed, in the office and the laboratory, on a regular basis.

In 1944, Frank died suddenly of a heart attack at the age of 59 and Tom became chairman and managing director. Shortly after his father's death, Geoff Cooper left the army to return to work at the undermanned brewery, becoming a director in 1945. Geoff eventually became chairman and managing director when Tom retired in 1969 and held the office of chairman until his retirement in 1989.

The lack of maintenance of the plant during the lean years of the Great Depression and World War II was taking its toll and there was an urgent need to update or replace ageing and run-down equipment. Although production began to rise after the war, a series of wage increases and continuing shortage of materials limited profits. However, by the mid-1950s, South Australia's population had grown significantly, wartime restrictions had all but vanished and the price of malt dropped. Profits began to rise again.

When Ray's son Maxwell, a fourth generation Cooper, joined the business in 1953 he became the first formally trained brewer at Cooper & Sons. After graduating from the University of Adelaide with a Bachelor of Science degree, Maxwell went to the UK to undertake a postgraduate course in malting and brewing at the University of Birmingham. He then took a position at W.B. Reid's brewery at Newcastle-on-Tyne, making him the first member of the Cooper family to have worked for another brewery.

With unprecedented training and experience, Maxwell returned full of ideas about improving practices at Cooper & Sons. The brewing process was labour intensive, production costs were increasing and Maxwell could see that the whole production process was inefficient. However, there was firm resistance from the board to any variation in brewing practices, which had remained largely unchanged for more than 70 years. The board's reluctance to make significant changes to practices that were recognised as obsolete by other breweries half a century prior, along with increasing wages, production costs and excise duty resulted in more than two decades of fluctuating sales and profits.

In 1955, an issue of additional shares to existing shareholders funded a new bottling line, but without substantial changes to production methods Cooper & Sons was just treading water and going nowhere.

Sink or swim

In 1962, rumours of potential takeovers of both SAB and Cooper & Sons by interstate and overseas breweries were circulating. The directors of Coopers met the board of SAB to discuss an arrangement that would allow the two companies to present a united defence against any takeover bid. The outcome of that meeting was an issue of Coopers shares that gave SAB a 25% interest in Cooper & Sons, along with the right to appoint one director to the board. In exchange, Coopers was granted a 2.65% interest in the much larger SAB. The arrangement was successful in discouraging takeover attempts.

The incoming fourth generation knew that consumer tastes were changing in favour of lighter beers and that the brewery needed to be modernised. In 1963, the board finally showed signs of following Maxwell's advice to produce a lager, but SAB was not happy about a product that would directly compete with its own. As a result, the innovation was deferred. Finally, in 1967, the board agreed to the brewing of lager. However, the production processes of lager are quite different from those used for ale and stout, which required substantial expenditure on a new building and equipment.

Maxwell was enlisted to develop the recipe for the new beer. Launched in September 1968, the lager, named Gold Crown, quickly captured the imagination of South Australian drinkers. SAB was not impressed by the new competition and refused to stock Gold Crown in its hotels, resulting in a four-year battle against Coopers before the Trade Practices Tribunal. The Tribunal ruled that SAB could not prevent the publicans of its hotels from selling Coopers Gold Crown lager. The successful production of this first lager demonstrated that Cooper & Sons was no longer totally reliant on its traditional ale and stout. It also provided incentive to produce more beers of a lighter style.

In mid-1969, the remaining third generation directors, Tom and Ray, resigned and were replaced by their respective sons, Bill and Maxwell. The board, apart from the SAB-appointed director Sir Norman Young, was now entirely in the hands of the fourth generation.

> Despite the entry into lager production and a new board, resistance to major changes in the production of ale and stout remained.

Despite the entry into lager production and a new board, resistance to major changes in the production of ale and stout remained. High labour and production costs continued to be a problem in the mid-1970s and an updated bottling line in a new packaging hall was created to reduce the need for overtime and shift work. However, for most of the 1970s, Cooper & Sons was playing catch-up with its competition by packaging in cartons for the first time, increasing production in cans and expanding its range of lagers.

In 1977, with inflation in double figures, higher taxes on beer, a restrictive regulatory environment and a slowing South Australian economy, it was clear that Cooper & Sons could not survive without a major overhaul of products, new markets and further cost-cutting in the brewery. The first step was the introduction of an ultra-low alcohol beer, Birell, under licence from the Swiss brewery Brauerei Hürlimann, now owned by Carlsberg. With less than 1% alcohol by volume, Birell attracted no beer excise and could be sold in supermarkets and delicatessens throughout Australia. Sales grew quickly and have been strong since. Birell is also exported to New Zealand.

Also in 1977, Maxwell Cooper was finally able to implement major changes in the brewing process – albeit slowly and cautiously. By 1982, Cooper & Sons had eliminated inefficient and labour intensive fermentation and yeast collection practices that should have ceased many years earlier, paving the way for long-term growth in production, sales and profits.

According to current managing director, Dr Tim Cooper, it was really home-brew that 'saved the company's bacon' when its future looked bleak. From the time that the Whitlam Government legalised the home-brewing of full-strength beer in 1973, the option of catering to the needs of home-brewers became apparent. Tim Cooper explains:

> 'By serendipity, brewer Ched Bolic had noticed that the dairy industry used 20 litre plastic bags to store milk.
> He set about finding out how it was done so that he could adapt it for storing wort.'

Wort is the liquid produced in the brewing process prior to fermentation.

Ched planned to use the stored wort for growing fresh batches of yeast. However, Maxwell and head brewer Paul

Berger immediately saw the potential of plastic bags of sterilised wort for home-brewing. After some experimentation they developed a home-brewing pack that included a 20 litre bag of wort and dried yeast. The packs were sold as Brewers Own Ale and allowed home-brewers to produce 26 standard sized bottles (750 ml) of full-strength ale at about one-third of the price of beer purchased in hotels and liquor stores. All the customers had to do was add yeast to the wort in a plastic container, ferment for a few days, add a little bit of sugar to stimulate the yeast when bottling and then wait for two weeks for maturation. Launched in October 1977, Brewers Own Ale packs became a runaway success and by the early 1990s, Coopers had become the largest manufacturer of home-brew kits in the world.

Coopers spreads its wings

Introducing Birell and home-brew packs to the market in the late 1970s had proved to be immensely successful. Under Bill's direction (he took over from Geoff as managing director in 1977), Coopers continued to pursue new markets and products. The company produced a draught beer for the first time in 1983; a lager, to increase its volume in hotels. However, it was not until 1987 that Coopers started producing naturally conditioned ale in kegs. In 1983, Coopers began supplying stout to Perth's Swan Brewery after its Kalgoorlie brewery shut down.

The drinking habits of Australians changed in the early 1980s as a result of drink-driving legislation and random breath testing in response to the growing road toll. Drinkers preferred to enjoy their bottled or canned beer at home rather than take the risk of driving to hotels to drink draught beer. Total beer consumption was in decline. The campaign against drink-driving had created a demand for low alcohol beers and Coopers wasted no time in launching Coopers Light, with an alcohol content of only 2.9% by volume. During the 1980s, the cost of low alcohol beers decreased as the government reduced the excise on these products, aiming to discourage the consumption of full-strength beer.

In 1980, the board decided that significant diversification was necessary to reduce reliance on the fickle beer market, which was still being plagued by government regulation and growing excise. That year, Coopers acquired a 15% interest in Adelaide Stereo, later Austereo, which was preparing to launch SAFM, Adelaide's first FM radio station. By the late 1980s, Austereo had acquired radio stations in Canberra and every mainland state of Australia and it was indeed a "sound" investment for most of that decade.

> In 1980, the board decided that significant diversification was necessary to reduce reliance on the fickle beer market, which was still being plagued by government regulation and growing excise.

Coopers engaged in a joint venture with two experienced maltsters in 1985, to establish Adelaide Malting Company Pty Ltd. A plant was built at Cavan, on the northern outskirts of Adelaide, to produce malted barley for brewing by Coopers and for export. The venture was an outstanding success, largely due to the quality of South Australian barley crops. Production doubled within the plant's first two years of operation and the plant had to be expanded to keep up with demand. By the early 1990s, Adelaide Malting was producing its internationally recognised malt for Asian breweries, including those operated by Heineken and Carlsberg.

In 1986, Coopers entered into a partnership to purchase and renovate Adelaide's historic Earl of Aberdeen Hotel. The refurbished hotel featured its own mini-brewery and was officially opened as the Coopers Alehouse in March 1987. Maxwell Cooper developed three new beers exclusively for sale in this hotel. One of those beers went on to become the highly successful Original Pale Ale. Although Coopers Alehouse was a huge success, the company's venture into three more hotels soon afterwards was less successful and they were sold by 1990. The Earl of Aberdeen was eventually sold in 1998 to help raise money for the construction of the new brewery at Regency Park.

Coopers entered into another partnership in 1989, acquiring an interest in the Panfida Foods manufacturing company, which produced breakfast cereals, biscuits, croissants, baking machinery and ovens. Coopers' share of the holding company, Premium Brands Pty Ltd, was 64%. However, it soon became apparent that Coopers had paid too much for the acquisition. Panfida was accused of overstating its earnings before the sale and Coopers sued the company for misrepresentation and deceptive conduct. However, Panfida Foods was placed in receivership before the proceedings against it commenced. An out-of-court settlement was reached in 1992, in which Coopers received a 91% majority interest in Premium Brands. Tim Cooper describes the investment in Panfida and involvement in Premium Brands as 'a tragedy that kept my father and the lawyers busy for years.' It took until 1998 before Coopers divested itself of all of its interests in Premium Brands.

Experiments in diversification continued in the 1990s, first with an investment in processing and packaging honey under the name of Leabrook Farms. This venture continued for 10 years. A joint venture with Inchcape Australia Ltd in 1994 to package Two Dogs alcoholic lemonade was a short-term success. Exports were strong but domestic sales, although initially promising, fell sharply. Coopers declined to invest further funds into promoting the brand.

A significant change occurred in 1988 when the name of the business was changed to recognise a female family member's involvement in the business. Bill's daughter Melanie, a chartered accountant with a degree in economics, had joined the business in 1985 as assistant to the company secretary. Cooper & Sons became Coopers Brewery Ltd. At board level, Geoff Cooper retired in 1989 and was replaced by Maxwell as chairman.

Innovation and growth

Maxwell and Bill understood that Coopers' future depended on the ability of the next generation to successfully manage and grow the business. They were both keen to ensure that family members of the next generation were given leadership positions in the business that matched their talents as early as possible. In 1993, Bill's son Tim Cooper was appointed as operations manager and also took over Maxwell's role as leading brewer, with the task of developing new and innovative beers as the ever-changing market demanded. At the same time, Tim's cousin Glenn was made responsible for beer sales and marketing. Both Tim and Glenn were to have a major influence on the future direction of the business.

The prelude to the innovation and growth that was about to take Coopers into the 21st century also occurred in 1993, when SAB was taken over by Lion Nathan. The New Zealand based company had already gobbled up Swan in Perth and Castlemaine Tooheys in Sydney and Brisbane. South Australian consumers were not at all impressed with their dominant local brewer being under the control of an overseas company. Coopers was quick to take advantage of the backlash and undertook an advertising campaign that portrayed its brewery as a South Australian icon.

With Coopers' beer sales improving and its growing range of products, it was clear that the brewing capacity of its brewery had to be expanded. But Leabrook was now a highly sought-after residential suburb and there was opposition from the local council to any further development. The neighbours were losing patience with the noise and traffic caused by the brewery. Also, by 1997, Coopers Distribution Centre in Norwood had run out of capacity after only 10 years of operation and there was no choice but to find a new location for the brewery, distribution centre and offices.

The search for a new, larger and less residential site for the brewery ended when Bill saw an advertisement in September

1997 for the Department of Transport's bus repair workshops at Regency Park, only six kilometres from the Adelaide CBD. After Coopers acquired the land, Tim spent the next three and a half years designing and building the new brewery and offices. In the meantime, the existing buildings were used for warehousing and distribution of products from Leabrook. The design, construction and transition from Leabrook tested the resolve of the Cooper family, employees and contractors.

The brewery of the future

The Regency Park brewery, officially opened in November 2001, is an intriguing fusion of innovation and Coopers' 19th century brewing traditions. It is considered the most technically and architecturally advanced plant of its kind in the world. The total cost was $40 million, which paid for cutting-edge equipment, a 4.4 megawatt natural gas powered cogeneration plant and a desalination plant designed by Tim and his team to produce adequate purified water through several bores about 200 metres below ground level. The quality of water is critical in the production of premium quality beers.

The Regency Park plant.

Shortly after the relocation to Regency Park, the Leabrook property was sold. The exceptionally successful Adelaide Malting was also sold to reduce the growing burden of debt. The sale included an agreement that allowed Coopers to purchase malt at a generous price for five years.

In early 2002, Maxwell stepped down as chairman and Glenn took over his role. Tim was appointed the new managing director. Bill remained on the board as a director and Cam Pearce, Maxwell's son-in-law, took Maxwell's seat on the board. Melanie Cooper returned to the company as financial accountant after having had a break to care for her family. With the move to Regency Park, and the fifth generation now managing the company, the transition for Coopers into a new and exciting era was complete.

The Golden Age begins

The relocation of Coopers to Regency Park presented numerous opportunities for innovation and expansion, and the fifth generation of the Cooper dynasty was well-qualified to take the company to unprecedented heights. In 2002, Budweiser approached Coopers through its distribution agent in Australia, Bruce Siney, owner of American Beverages Distributors Pty Ltd (ABD), to discuss a potential manufacturing licence. Bruce suggested to Tim that Coopers and ABD join forces to create an interstate sales joint venture. In October 2002, Glenn announced a joint venture company called Premium Beverages Pty Ltd, 'formed to service the needs of the Coopers and Budweiser brands'. Coopers held an 80% interest in the venture while ABD held the remaining 20%. Through the alliance, Coopers gained the opportunity to accelerate the growth of its own products interstate and internationally.

So successful was the venture that within two years the warehousing space at Regency Park had to be expanded and the volume of interstate sales of Coopers beer and partner brands grew from about 9 million litres to 60 million litres in the space of 15 years. In 2012, Coopers purchased Bruce Siney's 20% share and Premium Beverages became a fully owned subsidiary, with its head office in Port Melbourne.

In 2001, while the building at Regency Park was still in progress, Coopers acquired a 60% interest in Queensland-based Morgan's Brewing Co. Pty Ltd, the second largest Australian manufacturer of home-brew kits, behind Coopers. The former owners wanted to gradually exit the business over several years. Morgan's, now based in Yatala, Queensland, became a wholly owned subsidiary of Coopers Ltd in 2009.

Coopers purchased 80% of America's largest home-brew business, Mr Beer (based in Tucson, Arizona) in 2011, and the remaining shares in 2016. Also in 2011, Coopers signed an agreement to brew Japan's oldest beer, Sapporo. In the following year the company secured an agreement to brew Carlsberg and Kronenbourg 1664. By 2012, Coopers became Australia's largest remaining Australian-owned brewer.

Ambush!

On 1 September 2005, Lion Nathan Australia launched a hostile takeover bid for Coopers. Although the bid came as a shock to the directors, Coopers' relationship with Lion Nathan had been strained for over 10 years, since it took over SAB in 1993.

Prior to 1993, Coopers had been fighting SAB, unsuccessfully, for the right to use a certain refillable glass bottle. When Lion Nathan took over SAB, it wanted an interest in the Coopers shares that SAB had held since 1962. Lion Nathan suggested a proposal to allow Coopers to use the bottle in exchange for an interest in the shares. Coopers refused because its constitution required any available shares to be offered first to current shareholders.

Litigation was commenced in 1993 but an out-of-court settlement was reached soon after whereby Coopers was allowed to use a proprietary Lion Nathan non-refillable bottle in exchange for a change to Coopers' constitution. The change allowed Lion Nathan the right to purchase Coopers shares as long as they were offered first to Coopers' existing shareholders or their relatives, and second to AMP (as Coopers' superannuation trustee). The shares originally held by SAB were then purchased by existing shareholders and by the company. The constitutional changes effectively prevented any other brewer launching a takeover of Coopers.

After the takeover attempt of 2005 was launched, Tim and Glenn announced to the media that the board rejected the bid and that shareholders were opposed to the takeover. Coopers argued that the 1995 constitutional changes arising from the out-of-court settlement were no longer valid because Japanese food and beverage company Kirin had since gained a 45% controlling interest in Lion Nathan. There was a proviso in the constitution that, if there was 40% or more change in control of Lion Nathan, Coopers could seek to change its constitution to remove Lion Nathan's third tier option to purchase shares. In fact, litigation had been commenced in 2002 to effect this change to the constitution and the takeover bid was announced the day prior to judgment being delivered by the Supreme Court of South Australia.

Coopers was granted approval to allow its shareholders to vote on the change to the constitution. However, during the following two months there were bitter skirmishes between Lion Nathan and Coopers in the courts and in the media. Lion Nathan sought to delay or prevent the meeting of the shareholders by claiming that Coopers was discriminating against shareholders who wanted to sell and had not provided enough information for the shareholders to make an informed decision. Finally, in early December 2005, Coopers shareholders voted overwhelmingly at an Extraordinary General Meeting to remove the pre-emptive rights from the constitution, demonstrating their determination to maintain their brewing heritage for future generations. The matter didn't end there. It wasn't until October 2006 that Lion Nathan ceased all litigation.

Tim reflects on the Lion Nathan bid:

'We survived the takeover bid because we had a good legal defence and because most shares were in the hands of the fourth generation, who, in their 70s and 80s, didn't see the need to sell. They considered that it wasn't about the money, it was about keeping it in the family.'

He added:

'My father said, "I'm Bill Cooper of Coopers Brewery. If I sell my shares, I get $60 million. Who do I then become? Bill Cooper, owner of condominiums. What does that mean?"'

The Coopers community

Coopers has always valued its community of family members and employees. For more than 150 years it has been a proud member of the Adelaide and South Australian communities. Now, as the largest family-owned brewery in Australia, it is a widely recognised fixture in the Australian landscape.

In 2006, the company established the Coopers Brewery Foundation. Its stated aim is:

'to improve and protect the quality of life of Australians by providing support to charitable organisations with recognised strengths in medical research and health care, in youth education, and aged care, and in fostering family and community support, based on Christian values.'

Since it was established, the Foundation has contributed more than $5 million to over 200 charities. It is funded by activities at the brewery, including the proceeds of tours and concerts, as well as by speaker fees for Cooper family members, an annual golf day and donations from individuals and companies. Melanie chairs the Foundation and many other family members and employees donate time and services to help raise funds.

> **Check it out for yourself**
>
> Since the opening of the Coopers Museum in February 2006, guided tours of the brewhouse, bottling hall, onsite power station and museum have been one of Adelaide's "must-do" tourist attractions. Each tour concludes with a beer tasting in the museum. All of the pre-GST amount paid by visitors is donated to the Coopers Brewery Foundation.

Coopers' place in the community is well reflected in the awards won by both the business and family members. Among many other accolades in recent years, Coopers was named one of South Australia's 'icons' by the National Trust in 2003, the world's top family business by London-based family magazine *CampdenFB* in 2011 and Family Business of the Year by Family Business Australia in 2012.

Coopers takes its responsibility to the broader community seriously and is committed to reducing the amount of its waste going into landfill. All glass, cardboard packaging, aluminium and the metal components of old machinery are recycled. Grain and protein wastes are recycled as stock feed on farms surrounding Adelaide. Foundation Chair Melanie Cooper explains:

> 'We were spending money disposing of waste material to landfill and saw recycling as a way of reducing these costs. It became obvious that we could raise money through that recycling. We decided that all funds raised by recycling would go straight into the Coopers Brewery Foundation'.

Since the program was implemented, the amount of Coopers' waste going to landfill has been reduced by more than 40% and more than $680,000 has been raised for the Coopers Brewery Foundation.

Several members of the Cooper family have been recognised with Order of Australia honours. Bill Cooper OAM, Glenn Cooper AM, Dr Tim Cooper AM and Melanie Cooper AM have been honoured for a range of services to the brewing industry, the community, the environment and professional organisations. Glenn Cooper is chairman of Australian Made Campaign Limited, a not-for-profit public company that encourages consumers to buy Australian products and promotes Australian products at home and throughout the world. Tim has emerged as an industry leader, both in Australia and globally. In September 2018, he was appointed for a one-year term as President of the Institute of Brewing and Distilling, the largest global professional body representing brewers, distillers, maltsters and cider makers across 102 countries.

Reflections

Throughout the brewery's history, the Cooper family has maintained a strong bond with their employees, who now number approximately 230. Tim reflects:

> 'We have been privileged and fortunate over the decades
> to have the loyalty and long-term support of generations
> of employees, who have enabled Coopers to survive and
> grow, through their devotion to helping make the company
> a success.'

During the Great Depression, while many businesses sacked workers, Cooper & Sons, as it was then, retained them by reducing their working hours and rescheduling their shifts. Tim explains:

> 'We're historically reluctant to ask people to leave the
> business and when we've been through difficult times we've
> allowed the number of employees to decline by attrition.'

There has been a succession of loyal and respected employees who have remained with Coopers for many years. Numerous employees have brothers, sisters, sons, daughters or other relatives who have worked at the brewery.

Most of the joint ventures entered into by Coopers were either unsuccessful or short-lived. However, much was learnt from all of them. As Tim says:

> 'As a family business we can take a long-term view. Short-term crises are worth enduring for the sake of strengthening the family business.'

Tim credits his father Bill's generation with turning the company around after a long period of disappointing progress. He reflects:

> 'There is a feeling that the third generation were only able to maintain the brewery from before World War II until the end of the 1950s. There is no doubt that fourth generation Coopers, Maxwell and Bill, were responsible for turning the company around from the brink of collapse and setting it on a new course of modernisation and innovation.'

When Tim and Glenn joined the family business in 1990, over 60% of the brewery's beer sales by volume were in South Australia. Today, only 25% of Coopers beer is sold in South Australia. The remainder goes interstate or overseas. During the 20 years to 2017, a succession of production and profit records were broken, despite a significant reduction of overall beer production in Australia from 2010 onwards.

Coopers has raised its profile and brand awareness outside South Australia with clever marketing and sponsorship of events such as the Supercars series, the Australian Open tennis at Melbourne Park, the Woodford Folk Festival, the Sydney and Melbourne International Comedy Festivals, as well as the Adelaide Fringe Festival and WOMADelaide. The Coopers

Alehouse bar at Adelaide International Airport catches the eye of numerous interstate and international travellers.

Moving forward

The expense of the move to Regency Park and the investments in home-brewing certainly got Coopers off to an impressive start to the 21st century but the biggest investment in the company's history has been the $65 million malting plant, opened in 2017. Tim described the plant at its official opening as 'a state-of-the-art maltings with innovative design features and a strong focus on process control and hygiene'. Maltings manager Doug Stewart, with 18 years' experience in the maltings industry, even described the plant as 'beautiful'. It provides Coopers with a reliable source of high-quality malted barley at a lower cost. Two-thirds of the output is sold to other domestic breweries, including the craft beer market, or exported to Asia.

> Even founder Thomas Cooper recognised that being a son was not an entitlement to employment in the brewery and future partnership.

As the number of family members grew through the generations, the challenge of finding the right people to employ at the brewery and take on the responsibility of directorship became increasingly difficult. The handing down of the business from generation to generation was never automatic. Even founder Thomas Cooper recognised that being a son was not an entitlement to employment in the brewery and future partnership.

Both Glenn and Tim were discouraged in no uncertain terms from joining the family business by their fathers Ken and Bill respectively. Tim remembers a conversation with his father during his final year of high school in 1973, in which 'Dad asked what I was thinking of doing. I said Mechanical Engineering and then I'll go into the brewery. Dad said, "Oh no, you can't do that. The brewery is in the doldrums."' Glenn recalls a very similar conversation with his father when he left school. "Don't worry about the brewery," he said, "it won't make it."'

Following his father's advice, Tim completed a degree in Medicine at the University of Adelaide before moving to the United Kingdom where he was a registrar in medicine and cardiology in Bristol and Cardiff. He says:

> 'My sister Melanie had joined the business and my father suggested that I may like to be involved as well, given that the brewery was performing better. I studied brewing science at the University of Birmingham but still didn't feel ready to return to Adelaide and completed a Doctorate in Medicine at Bristol University.'

It wasn't until 1990 that Tim finally returned to join the business.

Glenn studied electronics and business management before working as a computer sales representative and eventually establishing his own successful computer business. When he was invited to join the family business in 1990, he had no hesitation in accepting the invitation and selling his business.

It is now well understood by the numerous descendants of Thomas Cooper that they will not be employed by the family business without adequate qualifications, experience elsewhere and a proven work ethic. Melanie was the first member of the fifth generation and first female member of the family to be approached to work in a permanent role in the company. She took Bill's place on the board in 2009 and is Director of Finance and Corporate Affairs as well as Company Secretary. Melanie says:

> 'One needs to have sufficient experience and service to warrant the appointment as a director and, going forward, as further female members of the family join the business, there will undoubtedly be further female director appointments.'

Glenn's daughter, Rachel Cooper-Casserly, became the first member of the sixth generation to work full-time at the brewery. Rachel joined the business as brand marketing coordinator in 2009 but has left the brewery to care for her family. She was followed by her younger brother Andrew, a former stockbroker with a Bachelor of Economics and an MBA, who joined the business as National Account Manager at Premium Beverages in Melbourne in 2017. Tim's daughter, Louise, joined the company in 2019 as Legal Affairs and Risk Manager. Other members of the sixth generation have worked at the brewery to fill short-term vacancies on a casual basis.

Coopers' ability to adapt to a volatile economic environment, changing tastes and decreasing demand for beer bodes well for the future. The ingenuity and resilience that goes right back to Thomas remains and a statement on the Coopers' website rings true:

'Our passion for brewing has kept us together and helped
us through economic recessions, wars, government imposts,
changing tastes, and the occasional hostile takeover bid.'

Information, photographs and materials included in this chapter have been extracted with permission from Jolly good ale and old: Coopers Brewery 1862–2012 *by Alison Painter, Tim Cooper and Rob Linn,* © *Coopers Brewery Limited, all rights reserved.*

CHAPTER 3

FURPHY

GOOD, BETTER, BEST

Photo on the previous page shows John Furphy's assistant Uriah Robinson on a Furphy's Farm Water Cart.

THE NAME FURPHY has been synonymous with the city of Shepparton in Victoria since blacksmith John Furphy moved his business there in 1873, nine years after opening his first workshop in Kyneton while still in his teens. He opened the business in Shepparton as a blacksmith and wheelwright shop before adding a foundry in 1878, an initiative which led to John Furphy becoming the region's largest manufacturer of agricultural machinery.

John Furphy's most famous product, the Furphy Farm Water Cart, invented in around 1890, achieved legendary status during World War I. Its use during the war made Furphy both a household name in Australia and a completely new word in the English-speaking world.

Furphy's is the oldest business in Shepparton and now operates as two separate companies located on adjoining sites sharing the same family heritage: J. Furphy & Sons and Furphy's Foundry. But as far as most of the locals are concerned it's just plain 'Furphy's'. John's business has now spanned three centuries and is still standing and thriving because his descendants have been successful in responding to social and technological change.

The beginning

John Furphy was born in the Melbourne suburb of Moonee Ponds in 1842, the eldest son of Irish immigrants Samuel and Judith Furphy. Shortly after John's birth the family moved to Yering Station in the Yarra Valley. When he reached school age he was home-schooled by his mother while his father worked as a gardener, dairyman and general hand. Educational resources were scarce, and his learning was most heavily influenced by the Bible and Shakespeare. John began his formal schooling at the age of eight when the family moved to Kangaroo Ground. The school had been established by Scottish Presbyterian settlers.

After only two years in Kangaroo Ground the family moved again, this time to the town of Kyneton in the Macedon Ranges, where Samuel opened a hay and corn store. After leaving school, John took on an apprenticeship as a blacksmith with a local manufacturer of ploughs, reaping machines and other farm machinery. By the time he completed his training in 1864, John Furphy knew exactly what he wanted to do with his life. He opened his own blacksmith shop in Piper Street, Kyneton, and within two years had married Irish-born Sarah Anne Vaughan and established his business well enough to necessitate a move to larger premises in the same street.

Strongly influenced by his mother's tutoring at Yering Station and his father's religious faith, hard work and resourcefulness, John grew up with sound moral values and a strong work ethic. As a young adult he became a devout Christian and retained his faith for the rest of his life.

By 1869, John's parents and siblings had all left Kyneton, establishing small farms on land selected by their father in the Lake Cooper district, about 100 kilometres north of Kyneton in the Goulburn Valley. John had no intention of abandoning his business, and remained in Kyneton until 1873. With the assistance of his sole employee Uriah Robinson, he supplied and repaired all types of farm machinery and took an interest in new inventions, including the bicycle, which had only recently appeared in Europe. John made at least two of these "new contraptions" before leaving Kyneton.

Greener pastures beckon

John Furphy was one of seven blacksmiths in Kyneton and, although his reputation of excellence in farm machinery manufacturing was strong, demand was limited, and he felt that there would be greater opportunities for his business in the Goulburn Valley. With his young assistant Uriah, John set out for the town of Mooroopna, on the banks of the Goulburn River, to search for a block of land on which to build a shop and dwelling.

On arrival in December 1873, he found land in Mooroopna to be too expensive and settled for a one-acre block across the river in the smaller town of Shepparton.

By the time John built his new blacksmith shop, the first in Shepparton, and cottage in 1874 he had been joined by his wife Sarah and their two surviving children, William and George, who had remained in Kyneton the previous year. Two other children, a daughter and a son, had tragically died in Kyneton during their infancy.

John Furphy's choice of location proved to be either fortuitous or remarkably astute – no one really knows which. Between 1871 and 1881 Shepparton's population grew from 33 to more than 1,000. A primary school, two banks and *The Shepparton News* were established during this period. Agricultural activity, especially wheat farming, had increased in the district and the railway line to Seymour had been extended to Shepparton.

John Furphy quickly became well known to farmers throughout the Goulburn Valley as a blacksmith, wheelwright and supplier of agricultural machinery, and was well respected in the Shepparton community. It wasn't long before Furphy's reputation for fine workmanship and reliable service spread beyond the Goulburn Valley, with orders coming in from farms in New South Wales. John Furphy's inventiveness resulted in patents for improved versions of a range of agricultural implements including grain strippers, disc harrows, ploughshares and toothed rollers.

By 1889, the business had grown from having a single employee, Uriah Robinson, who came with John Furphy from Kyneton, to one of the largest employers in the district, with 37 employees. John was lauded in the local newspapers as enterprising, perseverant, perceptive and confident. He was also recognised as a modest and unpretentious man of faith and integrity.

The Furphy Farm Water Cart

The most precious resource for farmers on the mostly dry Australian continent was, and still is, water. During the 19th century and the early part of the 20th century, the only way to take water to crops and stock was to transport it by horse and cart from rivers, creeks, lakes and dams. Even in larger towns, including Shepparton, before reservoirs and pipelines appeared, the precious liquid had to be carried by cart to water the streets to reduce dust and maintain gardens and lawns. The water carts built in Australia during the 1840s and 1850s consisted of a wooden barrel laid and strapped lengthwise on wooden shafts that could be harnessed to a horse. The barrels had a hole on top for filling and another for a tap or hose at the rear end.

John Furphy is believed to have been making simple water carts as a wheelwright since his arrival in Shepparton, but it wasn't until the addition of his foundry in 1878 that he possessed the resources to manufacture his own design, which eventually emerged in the early 1890s. John replaced the traditional wooden barrel with a galvanized iron tank bolted onto a wooden frame on wheels. The tank was fitted with an opening at the top for filling and cast iron ends with a tap at the rear end.

The first purpose-built Furphy's Farm Water Cart was produced around 1890. By 1895, the name Furphy was inscribed in prominent bold letters on both sides of the tanks and the name of the business, along with a list of its other products, was inscribed on each of the cast iron ends. Having been designed especially for local conditions, the Furphy carts provided a much better solution for farmers than the far more expensive imported alternatives.

The original 1895 tank end (at left) and the second version, with raised lettering and the addition of a verse at the bottom.

Good, better, best

A verse reflecting the philosophy and aspirations of John Furphy appears on the cast iron ends of every Furphy's Farm Water Cart manufactured from 1910:

Good, better, best,

Never let it rest;

Till your good is better,

And your better best.

Current managing director of J. Furphy & Sons, Adam Furphy, says, 'Having grown up with it, we have tended to take it for granted and perhaps underestimated its impact. However, it helped instil a terrific culture and is probably one of John Furphy's greatest gifts to the generations that followed.' The first line of the verse, and in some cases the whole verse, still appears on letterheads, logos, packaging, some products, websites and social media of both J. Furphy & Sons and the Furphy Foundry.

Generation two

In 1893 John Furphy brought his two older sons William and George into partnership, creating a J. Furphy & Sons. John's third son Frank showed no interest in the business and eventually moved to New South Wales as a farmer. Youngest son Charles began work in the foundry as a 14-year-old and was made a full partner after John's death in 1920. William and George had served their apprenticeships in the foundry and were well qualified to take the business into the approaching 20th century.

While remaining firmly in charge of the business, John gradually withdrew from the day-to-day management of the foundry and took great delight in conducting religious services at Methodist churches in and around Shepparton. He was also in high demand as a public speaker and chairman of social gatherings, able to engage his audiences with his confidence, his direct yet friendly approach and keen sense of humour.

John Furphy's announcement of the partnership with his older sons coincided with the peak of the depression of the 1890s, which forced the closure of more than half of Australia's banks and building societies. In turn, numerous farms and other businesses either struggled to survive or collapsed. Although J. Furphy & Sons was not immune to the effects of the depression, it was never in danger of having to close its doors. The water carts represented good value and were consequently less susceptible to the economic downturn than more expensive machinery, and the firm had established close relationships and loyalty with its long-standing customers and agents. J. Furphy & Sons was quick to protect itself and its employees by keeping its prices low or reducing them, shortening the working week from 54 to 48 hours when necessary and seeking new markets outside the Goulburn Valley.

With the depression over, in the last years of the 19th century there was increasing interest in Furphy's Farm Water Cart and on occasions the firm was unable to keep up with demand. There was no need for advertising in the press. The carts became indispensable and sold by reputation. And, of course, with the signage on the tanks they advertised themselves.

John Furphy's older sons, William and George, saw no need to change the business after their father's gradual withdrawal and eventual retirement. Like their father, they were generous and involved in the community. William seemed to inherit his father's sense of humour as well as his ingenuity and was not averse to expressing his opinion on the issues of his time, including government interference and transport. George followed in his father's footsteps as chairman of the Urban Water Trust. He was also president of the Shepparton Free Library and Workingman's Club.

Family discord

In 1883, John's younger brother Joseph fell upon hard times as a bullock driver in northern Victoria and the Riverina region of New South Wales. He accepted his brother's offer of a job in the foundry and housing for his whole family. Joseph's sons, Felix and Sam, took up apprenticeships in the foundry alongside their cousins, William and George.

Ten years later, Felix left Shepparton to start his own foundry across the river in Mooroopna. He was uncomfortable working for his uncle and cousins and felt the need to be independent. In 1897, when Felix persuaded his younger brother Sam to join him as a partner in his Mooroopna foundry, John Furphy angrily severed all business and personal connections with his nephews and banned them from entering his foundry 'either during or after working hours'.

Joseph Furphy, unlike his sons, enjoyed working with William and George. More importantly, his brother John gave him sufficient time off work to allow him to indulge in his love of writing. Joseph contributed stories and sketches to the popular and sometimes controversial magazine, *The Bulletin*, before writing a novel titled *Such is Life* under the pen name of Tom Collins, which he completed in 1897 and was finally published in 1903. *Such is Life*, inspired by his experiences in the bush and as a bullock driver, became an Australian classic. Joseph Furphy is now widely regarded as the father of the Australian novel.

In 1898, in what seemed to be an act of defiance, Felix and Sam moved their foundry across the river to Shepparton as Enterprise Foundry in direct competition with J. Furphy & Sons. Although their business name was different, they didn't hide their identity and called themselves Furphy Bros in their advertising. Naturally this caused some confusion among John Furphy's customers – especially as his nephews were manufacturing water carts and other farm machinery. Without the depth of experience and resources of John Furphy, Enterprise Foundry was unable to withstand the severe drought of 1902 and was forced to close and relocate under a new owner.

Six months later, J. Furphy & Sons purchased the relocated Enterprise Foundry on the condition that Felix and Sam were not to open any opposition business in Victoria or the Riverina. There was now only one Furphy's in Shepparton. Whether the locals called it Furphy's Foundry, J. Furphy & Sons or just plain Furphy's no longer mattered. In a remarkable gesture of family loyalty, John Furphy provided financial support to allow Felix and Sam to establish a foundry in Fremantle, which they operated until they sold it in 1939.

By 1906, J. Furphy & Sons had moved to a larger site in Hoskins Street, which was closer to the railway line. Hugh McKay's famous Sunshine harvester was dominating the market. John Furphy could not compete with McKay's invention and ceased manufacturing his own harvesters, but his farm water cart was so well established that rival foundries trying to compete failed miserably. J. Furphy & Sons also supplied farm ploughs, rollers, cultivators, farm gates and numerous other farm machines and castings.

John Furphy finally retired in 1909 and, with his wife Sarah, moved to the Melbourne suburb of Albert Park, where they lived with their daughter Harriet. He died of a heart attack in September 1920 at the age of 78.

Furphy becomes a household name

The name Furphy was already well known throughout northern Victoria before World War I broke out. But it was the use of the horse drawn Furphy Farm Water Cart during World War I that made it a household name throughout the nation. Before the war was over, stories about the Furphy water carts delivering water to the troops in the trenches of Gallipoli and the deserts of Egypt had reached Australians at home through newspapers and magazines. In the years following the war, the name Furphy was recognised by most Australians to an extent that advertising could never achieve.

The origin of the word 'furphy'

Since its first use during World War I, the word 'furphy' has been included in English dictionaries throughout the world. At Lexico.com (a collaboration between Dictionary.com and Oxford University Press), furphy is defined as *'a rumour or story, especially one that is untrue or absurd'.*

South Australian Member of Parliament Captain W. J. Denny, who served in Egypt and France during World War I and was awarded the Military Cross, provided an explanation of the origin of the word furphy in his book *A Digger at Home and Abroad*, published in 1941. He wrote, 'The drivers of water carts bearing that name in early Australian camps and even at Gallipoli alleged to spread news of future troop movements and camp gossip, usually far-fetched and inaccurate.'

Although Denny's statement is partially correct, it is believed that 'furphy' first became associated with rumours and gossip in the Broadmeadows camp near Melbourne where soldiers were waiting to be transported to serve abroad. Water had to be carted into the Broadmeadows camp because it was not connected to the Melbourne metropolitan supply. Soldiers would congregate eagerly around the arriving water carts, with the name Furphy prominently painted on both sides of the tanks, to hear 'the latest news' from the drivers, who would often exaggerate, provide reports of doubtful accuracy, or even make up mischievous tales about the war.

Another version of the origin says that soldiers gathering around the carts near the latrines would swap stories and embellish them along the way. In fact, the water carts used in Gallipoli and elsewhere were supplied by H. V. McKay and Lawtons to an unbranded military specification. However, as a result of the Broadmeadows experience the horse drawn carts were already known as Furphys.

William Furphy, as inventive as his father, had been developing a new range of water carts for several years before the outbreak of war in 1914, each one suited for specific purposes. The Furphy No. 6, like the original, had two wheels but was fitted with pneumatic tyres and a chassis that made it suitable for towing at higher speeds by a tractor or truck. Another version, the Furphy No. 8, was mounted on hardwood bearers that could be mounted on a trailer or the back of a truck. This version was used extensively by bush fire brigades.

New challenges: the Great Depression and World War II

The business continued to thrive under the leadership of John Furphy's sons. William managed the foundry and administration while George managed heavy implement manufacture and repairs. Younger son Charles worked at the foundry as a fitter and turner. William had an aversion to what he called 'excessive profits' and this kept prices low, sales steady and customers happy in the lead up to the Great Depression.

By 1927, three of John Furphy's grandsons had entered the business. Fred, William's eldest son, came to the foundry in 1922 as a qualified engineer with expertise in the new techniques of electric welding. Albert, William's second son, joined the business four years later as an accountant and administrator. George's only son, John Seeley Furphy, known as Jack, started working in the foundry as a boy after school, where he painted the name Furphy on the sides of the water carts.

In 1929, J. Furphy & Sons transformed itself from a partnership to a private company with third generation Fred, Albert and Jack, along with second generation William, George and Charles as directors. There was little change in the business as the depression approached. The Furphy's Farm Water Cart remained the company's most profitable product; however, sales decreased from 274 in 1929 to 51 in 1934, indicating the impact of the economic downturn on both the business and the surrounding rural communities. Sales of all other Furphy's large farm implements also dropped dramatically. Yet there was still enough work to keep the business going and retain most of the staff.

Having kept as many employees as possible, the business was in a strong position to recover when the Great Depression ended and the demand for farm machinery and water carts returned. Before the outbreak of World War II, the number of Furphy Farm Water Carts sold had rebounded to more than pre-depression levels.

By the time World War II began in 1939, J. Furphy & Sons was in a strong financial position and any fear that the war would threaten it was short-lived. The company was classified as a "protected industry" because of the need for water carts, machine gun mountings and supplies of castings for Melbourne foundries that could not supply the Department of Defence quickly enough.

William Furphy was concerned that there would be a slump in business when the war was over, but it didn't eventuate. The Goulburn Valley had a bright future in agriculture after the war and the foundry remained as busy as ever, with the switch from making implements of war back to agricultural machinery.

Reinventing the business

All three second generation directors passed away during the 1950s: William in 1953 at the age of 86, George in 1955 at the age of 84 and Charles in 1959 at the age of 79. All shares were now in the hands of John Furphy's grandsons Fred, Albert and Jack, who were the sole directors of the company.

In 1960, Fred and Jack Furphy were still working at the foundry while Albert, having recovered from serious lung surgery, had turned to farming beef cattle not far from Shepparton. Neither of William's sons, Fred or Albert, had male heirs. Jack, who had four sons, acquired the shares of both of his cousins, becoming sole owner and ending the involvement of William's line of the family in the business.

Following the buyout Jack was in control of the business and cousin Fred managed operations at the foundry. However, when Fred died suddenly of a heart attack in 1961, aged 61, Jack's eldest son Roger – who had yet to complete his apprenticeship as a moulder in Melbourne – returned to Shepparton to take charge of the foundry from the floor. Demand for traditional products such as the water carts, troughs, spike rollers and pig troughs was in decline and it was Roger's responsibility to find new work and new customers. His son Sam, current managing director of Furphy's Foundry, recalls:

> 'Dad acquired new equipment for the foundry and new customers such as the Weights and Measures Board, State Rivers and the Sydney Harbour Water Authority. As well as undertaking these contracts he manufactured domestic products such as the Furphy Pot Belly and Dover Stoves, lacework and balustrades. Hall and umbrella stands and garden furniture were added to the range of products later.'

Jack's second son Andrew joined the business in 1962 after completing an apprenticeship as a fitter and turner in Melbourne. He managed general engineering and sheet metal production, which was expanding with an increasing demand for stainless steel equipment from the food processing and wine industries in the Goulburn Valley. When Jack's third son Timothy followed into the business in 1969, he worked closely with Andrew to help manage general engineering and the growing production of stainless steel.

By 1970, Jack's three eldest sons had been appointed as directors. His youngest son Simon studied law and practised in Shepparton, where he lived until his death in 2014. Jack's only daughter Antoinette was a shareholder but took no active role in the business.

Throughout its history, most of Furphy's customers were individual farmers, usually placing one or two products per order. During the 1960s and 1970s, there was an increasing demand for the supply of multiple items to other companies and government institutions, which often required quoting or tendering and a more formal approach to administration. The company was expanding rapidly and 1978 it had no choice but to move to a new and larger site on the New Dookie Road. Existing and expanding Shepparton businesses such as SPC and Campbell's Soups, along with customers from Melbourne and interstate, provided an unprecedented demand for Furphy engineering and stainless steel.

In 1983, production of the traditional Furphy's Farm Water Cart, with its legendary cast iron ends, finally ceased. This marked the end of a remarkable era for J. Furphy & Sons. The traditional cart was replaced with a fully galvanized Furphy Water Tank, which is lighter, stronger and resistant to corrosion. Just one year later, the first galvanizing plant in Australia away from the coast was constructed on the New Dookie Road site. A fully owned subsidiary of J. Furphy & Sons, it began as Goulburn Valley Galvanizing and now trades as Furphy Galvanizing.

The fork in the road

In the early 1980s, with the emergence of Chinese imports of cast iron products and decreasing production costs for local

competitors due to automated machinery, the foundry operations required a significant investment in the automation of
equipment. At the same time, with management focusing on
new opportunities in engineering and sheet metal, J. Furphy
& Sons was slowly transforming itself into two separate and
quite distinctive businesses. A major investment in foundry
automation was ultimately not seen as a worthwhile investment.
However, Roger Furphy felt that the foundry operations had the
potential for a bright future, although the exact nature of new
initiatives had yet to be clearly identified.

The decision of how to move forward was an agonising one
for brothers Roger and Andrew. Younger brothers Timothy and
Simon, and sister Antoinette, took no part in the discussion.
Timothy had left the business in 1977 to establish a John Deere
outlet in Shepparton. There was a lot at stake, with more than a
hundred years of history behind the business and future generations of the Furphy family to consider. In an amicable settlement
in 1989, Furphy's Foundry was separated from J. Furphy & Sons
and formally established in its own right. Roger became the
sole owner of Furphy's Foundry and Andrew the sole owner of
J. Furphy & Sons, which included engineering and galvanizing
operations. At about the same time, Furphy's Foundry won a
project with the Benalla Shire Council to produce a range of cast
iron public seats, benches and bollards, which would ultimately
set the new direction for the foundry operations to this day.

The cousins

Thirty years after the split, cousins Sam and Adam Furphy are
the custodians of the history and heritage of the Furphy family
business. Sam is the son of Roger Furphy and managing director
of Furphy's Foundry. Adam is the son of Andrew Furphy and
managing director of J. Furphy & Sons. The companies operate
on adjoining sites in Drummond Road, Shepparton.

Sam was in his final year of school at Geelong Grammar when the split occurred. His cousin Adam was two years behind at the same school. They both remember it being a very difficult time for their respective fathers.

Adam joined J. Furphy & Sons as managing director when his father Andrew retired in 1998. Adam had completed a Bachelor of Engineering (Mechanical) at RMIT in 1995 and worked in the power industry for 18 months. However, he had no experience in the family business apart from casual work as a youngster during the school holidays. Adam recalls:

> 'I was given responsibility as managing director early on in my time with the company, which was daunting. But in hindsight it was a great opportunity. My father engineered this and, whilst it was a risk, there were a good number of experienced staff members who made the process easier than it might have been.'

He believes that some of those employees could have run the business. 'That can be attributed to Dad's knack of picking the right person for each job and just letting them roll up their sleeves get on with it,' says Adam.

Andrew firmly believed that his employees and family would perform best when presented with opportunities. Although he handed over the reins to his son, he still had a presence. Adam reports:

> 'There were lots of tough conversations in the early years, which frustrated both of us. I often thought to myself during these times that, whilst I found it frustrating, my father probably had the harder part of it given that he had put so much of himself into the business over the years. But, although we didn't always see eye to eye, we managed to navigate the process together pretty well.'

Sam Furphy (right) and Adam Furphy (left) in front of the Furphy Museum in Shepparton.

Sam had a very different entry to the business. After completing school, he studied business marketing at Swinburne University of Technology before working in the motor auction industry as an account executive. In 1993, at the age of 23, Sam joined the Furphy's Foundry business, operating a new retail outlet in Prahran called Furphy Ironworks, selling ornate cast iron reproductions such as lacework and garden furniture. The shop doubled as an office for Sam's main focus, which was the sale and marketing of street and park furniture to councils, schools and architects.

Sam recounts his father Roger's retirement:

'Dad was still involved but was planning his exit. As much as he had the door open for me, we had plenty of young bull–old bull kitchen table conversations. I think it was hard on my mother more than anyone else.'

Since the split in 1989, J. Furphy & Sons has transformed itself into a group of companies made up of Furphy Engineering, Furphy Galvanizing, Geelong Galvanizing and Albury Galvanizing. The J. Furphy & Sons Group employs a total of more than 180 people across its sites in Shepparton, Geelong and Albury. The three galvanizing plants provide corrosion protection services for fabricators and equipment manufacturers throughout Victoria and New South Wales. Furphy Galvanizing in Shepparton, the first of the galvanizing plants, was built in 1984 and supports fabrication by both Furphy Engineering and Furphy's Foundry in addition to a wide customer base in northern Victoria.

Today, Furphy Engineering specialises in fabricating stainless steel tanks, heat exchange systems and pressure vessels. The company is at the forefront of laser welding with its latest investment in a dedicated laser welding machine. Furphy Engineering has fabricated stainless steel tanks for a range of companies including Campbell's Soups, Shepparton Preserving Company (SPC), Commonwealth Serum Laboratories, Masterfoods, Nestlé, Kimberly-Clark and Wattyl Paints. Furphy Engineering's tanks include some giants, such as a 600,000 litre spray drier vessel fabricated in 2003 and transported in a single piece to a Melbourne manufacturer of adhesives and tile grout. The vessel was 20 metres long with a diameter of 6.2 metres and weighed about 17 tonnes. The journey from Furphy Engineering in Shepparton to its destination in Melbourne took several days and required a convoy of escort vehicles.

More recently, a major investment in expanded and automated facilities has allowed the completion of much larger projects such as a recent project for more than 40 beer fermenters, ranging in capacity from 80,000 to 100,000 litres. With a large workforce of metal tradesmen, Furphy Engineering has also been a significant provider of apprenticeships in Shepparton over the last three decades, with an ongoing commitment of 10 to 20 apprentices at any one time.

Roger Furphy's faith in the ability of the foundry to be invigorated was vindicated soon after the split. Sam Furphy explains:

'Roger identified a heightened focus of councils seeking to implement more architecturally designed street and park furniture products. Foundry castings enabled superior designs, which laid the foundations for the foundry operations as they stand today.'

Within a few years of joining the family business, Sam took responsibility for the strategy of the foundry and oversaw a major change from cast iron production to cast aluminium production. He also introduced new moulding techniques in the steel fabrication division to broaden the product offering. When the newly elected Kennett Government introduced compulsory competitive tendering in 1994, Sam saw an opportunity to not only sell street furniture, but to install and maintain it. He recalls:

'I scratched out a business plan over two nights, borrowed $5,000 from the foundry and established Urban Maintenance Systems, a fully owned subsidiary of Furphy's Foundry.'

The new subsidiary quickly won long-term contracts with several city councils to supply and maintain roadside furniture assets and over a 20-year period became a leading provider of infrastructure and facility management services throughout Australia, employing 380 staff.

By the late 1990s, a new challenge emerged for the foundry as Roger was reducing his day-to-day involvement and Sam was focused on managing Urban Maintenance Systems. To ensure the smooth running of the foundry, Sam and Roger established an advisory board, which included two external advisors, to focus on corporate governance, strategy and performance. 'We recruited a new manager to oversee the day-to-day operation of the foundry. As the business grew, a small and capable management team enabled Roger to remove himself from foundry operations and me to run Urban Maintenance Systems,' says Sam.

In 2012, Furphy's Foundry acquired Landmark Products Pty Ltd, a national design, manufacturing and installation organisation specialising in the production of open space structures that are found in most local parks. Products such as restrooms, shelters, pedestrian bridges and boardwalks have complemented Furphy's Foundry's core product offering of street and park furniture. Today, the Furphy Foundry Group (including Landmark) employs 75 full-time staff

> Although our businesses operate on a national, and in some cases international scale, our heartbeat is in Shepparton.

and is a truly national business, with offices in each capital city and representation in New Zealand and the United Arab Emirates. Sam sold his shareholding in Urban Maintenance Systems in 2014 'because of the intense competitive landscape and to focus on developing the Furphy Foundry Group for the next generation'.

The Shepparton community

There is no doubt that Shepparton's growth and prosperity has played a very significant part in the success of J. Furphy & Sons and Furphy's Foundry. The reverse is also true and Shepparton continues to benefit from the contributions of the Furphy businesses. As Sam Furphy says, 'Although our businesses operate on a national, and in some cases international scale, our heartbeat is in Shepparton.'

John Furphy, his son George, grandson Fred and great grandson Roger all served on the Urban Water Trust, of which John was inaugural chairman. The management of water and irrigation has been critical in the development of the Goulburn Valley. Fred was a strong advocate of technical education and was instrumental in establishing Shepparton Technical School. The family has made numerous contributions to the Shepparton Heritage Centre Museum, established in 1972. Roger Furphy became the first member of the family to be elected to Shepparton City Council and served as Mayor in 1984. In the following year, he chaired the Shepparton Sesqui-centenary Committee. Both J. Furphy & Sons and Furphy's Foundry have continued the long-standing Furphy tradition of enthusiastically supporting many local charity organisations and initiatives as well as sporting and social clubs.

Reflections

In 1973, the 100th anniversary of John Furphy's arrival in Shepparton, his grandson Jack paid tribute to his grandfather in a booklet published to celebrate the occasion:

> 'Our firm has not lasted for a hundred years by accident or by luck. It can be directly related to the strength and genius of John Furphy and the solid foundations he laid for us.'

Almost 50 years on from that anniversary, John Furphy's legacy lives on and his family business, with a very different structure, is stronger than ever with his great, great grandsons Adam and Sam Furphy building new foundations for future generations.

When John Furphy opened his blacksmith shop in Kyneton in 1864 he worked alone and by the time he moved to Shepparton nine years later his only employee, Uriah Robinson, went with him. The mutual sense of loyalty between John and Uriah all those years ago has continued through the subsequent generations of Furphys; the relationship between management and staff remains close.

Adam Furphy says, 'A lot of the staff love the fact that they work for a family business. And we've had a few generations of the same family working for us.' He remembers that the period of transition from his father's management tenure to his own took some time and was obviously of interest to the employees – many of whom had been working with the company for many years. 'I have to say, I felt very supported by the staff despite them perhaps having their reservations about the unknown.'

Sam Furphy described the knowledge and skills of the staff in his early days as that of true craftsmen and fondly remembers presenting a 50-year certificate to an employee who started working at the foundry in the same year as his father. The longest-serving employee is believed to be a blacksmith named Donald Douglas who worked at the foundry for 60 years.

There is no longer a board of directors at either J. Furphy & Sons or Furphy's Foundry. The strategic direction of the companies is determined by Adam and Sam respectively. Adam found that having managers as directors was not effective. 'As managing director, I was chairing a board made up of my management team – it didn't really work for me despite having worked for my father,' he says. Adam's aim was to establish good connections with external independent advice and a strong and engaged management team. He explains:

'My view is that the management team should drive the business at a mutually formed direction. My job is to incentivise them and encourage them to act in the best long-term interest of the business.'

His cousin Sam reflects on his responsibility as managing director without a board:

'If the management team is unable to resolve a conflict the ultimate responsibility falls to me as managing director.'

The name and heritage of Furphy is indelibly associated with the legendary Furphy's Farm Water Cart with the name Furphy emblazoned on the sides in big capital letters and its cast iron ends. The cast iron tank ends, and the carts themselves, are sought-after collectors' items. There have been about 25 variations of the ends over the years and they can sell from about $750 up to more than $17,000 for the rarer versions. Since the last traditional Furphy's Farm Water Cart was built in 1983, there have been several commemorative castings of the tank ends, including a limited edition release in 1998 of 21 numbered ends to celebrate the 125th anniversary of John Furphy's arrival in Shepparton. A whole commemorative tank was built for the 150th anniversary of the founding of Shepparton. There is an active collectors' group, whose members keep a keen eye on farm clearance sales.

A limited edition tank end manufactured by Furphy's Foundry and J. Furphy & Sons in cast aluminium and released in early 2019. A new design reflects the current day activities of both companies. The tank ends are individually numbered with numerals cast on the reverse side and accompanied by a certificate of authenticity signed by Sam and Adam Furphy. Prices currently range from $1,100 to $1,650.

The tank ends

People often ask about the mysterious markings across the middle of the tank ends, which some mistake as a message in Arabic. The markings present a message written in Pitman shorthand, a notation used by secretaries and journalists for recording verbal statements quickly.

The first inscription was chosen by William Furphy and reads, *'Water is the gift of God, but beer is a concoction of the devil. Don't drink beer'*, which reflects William's Methodist faith and his distain for alcohol. The inscription was later extended to read, *'Water is a gift from God, but beer and whiskey are concoctions of the devil. Come and have a drink of water.'*

A cast iron Furphy tank end, now located on a wall in Australia's Parliament House near the press gallery, formerly adorned the non-Members' (Journalists') bar in the same building, an ironic location given the message it bears.

The Furphy heritage was always an important consideration in the management of the business. It was a key factor in Jack's buyout of his cousins in 1960 and the split of John Furphy & Sons into two separate companies in 1989. Adam and Sam Furphy agree that regardless of the structure and administrative processes, both companies are custodians of the family history, heritage and legacy. Adam explains:

> 'Although we are now two separate businesses, we share the Furphy name and have a common duty to previous generations to encapsulate the stories and make it easy for people to access them.'

The cousins' commitment to preserving the family history and heritage was well illustrated when they worked together to establish the Furphy Museum, located at Shepparton Motor Museum, in 2014. The museum includes a replica of John Furphy's original Kyneton blacksmith and wheelwright business, and numerous examples of Furphy agricultural implements and water carts. The museum traces over 150 years of the history of the business established by John Furphy in 1864.

The history and heritage of the Furphy family has also been preserved in print. Roger Furphy tells the story of John and Joseph Furphy in the biography *Two Brothers: A Bit of a Yarn* (published in 1996 by Primavera Press). A book entitled *Made in Shepparton: The History of J. Furphy & Sons 1873–1998*, written by John Barnes, was published by J. Furphy & Sons in 1998 in celebration of 125 years in Shepparton. It includes contributions by Andrew and Adam Furphy. In 2005, John Barnes and Andrew Furphy documented the history of Furphy's Farm Water Cart and the origin and development of the word furphy in *Furphy: The Water Cart and The Word* (published by Australian Scholarly Publishing).

It's a furphy

The launch of Furphy Beer in 2014 has added a completely new dimension to the Furphy heritage. It is, in fact, a furphy that the ale is brewed by Furphy's of Shepparton. It was developed by Little Creatures in Geelong especially for the Victorian market. The brewer was seeking a truly Victorian brand name. The choice of name came about when the owner of Little Creatures spotted a Furphy logo on an invoice for their new stainless steel beer fermenters for their new brewery in Geelong. An agreement to use the Furphy name and heritage to market the beer was reached.

Moving forward

According to Adam Furphy, the future of both J. Furphy & Sons and Furphy's Foundry depends on their ability to continue to adapt to both changes in materials technology and a changing marketplace. The Furphy products of today differ vastly from the cast iron inventions and adaptations of John Furphy. 'But the values of John Furphy encapsulated in the words "Good, better, best" remain,' Adam says.

Adam and Sam Furphy are totally committed to setting up the business for the next generation and beyond. However, there is no formal succession plan. Adam says, 'I think our forebears have been pretty good at doing what is best for the business. Looking after the business gives you options.' Both businesses are well aware of the contribution made by non-family members and want to ensure that they are provided with opportunities for meaningful participation in management.

Sam has three sons, while Adam has two daughters and a son. Sam predicts, 'It is likely that Furphy's Foundry will be managed by all or one of my sons Tom, Hamish or Gus.' He hopes that the business will be diverse enough to offer rewarding employment opportunities to the next generation but concedes that it is possible that one or more of his sons might not join the business. Adam shares his view: 'I don't want to put pressure on the kids to be involved but it would be great if one or more of them were interested. It's definitely not for everyone and if their interest lies elsewhere then so be it,' he says. Sam believes that even without pressure there is an underlying sense of obligation. 'I had it,' he says, 'even though my father said, "If you're not interested, do your own thing mate".' Adam is keen to explore how the families can remain involved without being employed in the business.

The split of the business into two provided some lessons about succession for Adam and Sam. They both remember the stress and anxiety that their parents went through. Adam says:

'Roger and Andrew had different ideas, skills and areas of interest. They both made decisions, however, that were ultimately good for the family and the businesses.'

Furphy's Foundry supplies products to New Zealand and the United Arab Emirates, with plans underway to export to North America. There is also potential for expansion in South East

Asia. Adam and Sam agree that it is important to spot opportunities and capitalise on them, as J. Furphy & Sons has already done with galvanizing and Furphy's Foundry has done with open space structures. 'As a multi-generational family business, you have to think about what the business will look like 20 years from now,' says Sam Furphy. 'We have learnt from our forefathers that adapting to emerging opportunities and markets is a key ingredient for sustained success.' Adam hopes that 20 years from now the Furphy business will have expanded both its scope of services and operating locations. 'We want both businesses to continue to exist and thrive into the future, providing meaningful employment for their employees and satisfaction and financial rewards for shareholders, many of whom are descendants of our founder John Furphy,' says Adam.

> We have learnt from our forefathers that adapting to emerging opportunities and markets is a key ingredient for sustained success.

CHAPTER 4

DYMOCKS

LEARNING FOR LIFE
WITH BOOKS

Photo on the previous page is of the entrance to the Dymocks flagship store in George Street, Sydney.

WHEN WILLIAM DYMOCK opened his first bookstore in a rented room in Sydney, he was still in his late teens. The year was 1879, the population of Sydney was just over 200,000 and the fastest mode of transportation in the city was horse and cart. In the 140 years since, in a vastly different world, William's modest business has grown into Australia's largest bookseller, with more than 60 stores across every state and territory of the nation and a website that attracts an average of more than 22,500 visitors per day.

The Dymocks of today has a strong commitment to improving the literacy of young Australians. It does this through its network of locally owned and operated stores and its charity, Dymocks Children's Charities, which provides literacy support programs designed to improve the lives of children by cultivating better reading skills.

Dymocks bookstores represent the largest and best-known component of what has grown into the Dymocks Group, which employs about 2,500 Australians. The group has a range of interests including property and other investments, education, aviation, macadamia farms, high-end stationery and lifestyle products.

A modest beginning

William Dymock, the fourth son of Scottish immigrants, was born in Melbourne in 1861. When his family moved to the Sydney suburb of Redfern several years later, he attended Cleveland Street Public School before obtaining a job, while still a young lad, as an assistant in a bookstore. William worked in two other bookstores before beginning his own bookselling business in a rented room in Market Street, Sydney in 1879.

William had already become aware of the value of old Australian books and developed a passion for obtaining rare books for discerning collectors, including David Scott Mitchell, who donated his entire collection to the Public Library (now State Library) of New South Wales before his death.

William had no employees and ran the business alone, selling books to libraries, searching for manufacturers who needed technical books and sourcing books suitable for his individual customers. He travelled to Europe three times to purchase entire collections and obtain rare books on behalf of the Booksellers Association of Australia and other collectors.

By 1881, William's business had outgrown that small upstairs room in Market Street and he moved to a shop at 208 Pitt Street, which he named Dymock's Book Arcade. Further growth necessitated another move, this time to 142 King Street, before the final move to the Royal Hotel building at the current site of the Dymocks Building at 428 George Street in 1890. William advertised his relocated Dymock's Book Arcade as the largest bookshop in the world with more than one million books in stock.

In his book *Old Books, Old Friends, Old Sydney*, James Tyrrell reports that it was William's 'aggressive sales techniques' that forced him to expand. William Dymock was an astute businessman and invested in valuable library collections. He believed that books were to be browsed through and open to inspection by the public. Tyrrell comments:

> 'He pioneered the concept of lots of glass and walk-in shopping; a concept to become known as the shopping arcade.'

There was a friendly but vigorous rivalry between William Dymock and George Robertson, who had partnered with David Angus in 1886 to form Angus & Robertson. William and George had worked together at a bookstore before William formed his own business. George Robertson described his friend as 'the somewhat erratic but wholly lovable William Dymock'. William had the distinction of being the first Australian-born owner of a successful and enduring bookselling business. In addition to being a leading bookseller, Dymocks was a major publisher of Australian works until 1960, when the company decided to focus entirely on retailing.

There is no evidence to suggest that the depression of the 1890s had any impact on William's business. In fact, his stock and profits continued to grow. His fascination with rare books may have given him some immunity from the effects of the depression.

Sadly, William Dymock died of a brain haemorrhage in October 1900 at the age of only 39. The shock of his sudden and unexpected death was felt across the whole Sydney community as well as by his family. William was much liked and respected within the Sydney community. He was a prominent and well-respected member of the bookselling fraternity. Two years before his death, he had been elected as an Alderman to Sydney Municipal Council, having campaigned vigorously as a young, broad-minded Australian with progressive views.

William was unmarried and had no children, so the business was inherited by his sister Marjory Forsyth. Marjory's son, John Malcolm Forsyth, had started working for William Dymock as a general assistant at an early age, reportedly as a 14-year-old, and had learnt all aspects of the business, right down to sweeping the floor. It was not surprising that John Malcolm was appointed by his mother as manager of her late brother's bookselling business. By the time he was 22 years old he was managing director and chairman of Dymocks Book Arcade. Since then, Dymocks has been managed by the Forsyth family.

The Block

Dymocks had been a tenant in the Royal Hotel building since December 1890 and, as the business had continued to grow and prosper, John Malcolm decided to buy the property in 1922 for further expansion and investment. The five-storey building, which was once the tallest building in Sydney, was demolished in 1925 to make way for a new 11-storey Art Deco Palazzo-style building to house the street-level book arcade and entice specialty businesses as tenants to the upper floors.

Work on the present Dymocks Building commenced in or just before 1926, but completion was delayed as a result of the early part of the Great Depression in 1930. John Malcolm decided to issue preference shares through the stock market to help keep Dymocks afloat during the downturn and ensure that the building was completed. Dymocks moved in before the building, initially known as 'The Block', was finally completed in 1932.

Attracting tenants to the new 11-storey building at the height of the Great Depression was going to be a challenge, but as the current owner and chairman John Pemberton Curlewis Forsyth explains:

> 'During the depression it was generally hard to get tenants, but as a vertical retail building, with wide shopping arcades, rent was cheaper in the upper levels of the Dymocks Building because there was no street frontage apart from the book arcade.'

During World War II, and for many years after, most of the building was leased to various government departments for office space. It wasn't until the late 1980s, when the building was restored, that the upper floors were finally occupied by the tenants for which it was designed.

The Block today

The Block is now one of the most architecturally and historically significant buildings in the Sydney CBD, and home to more than 130 specialty stores and businesses, specialising in fashion, jewellery, wedding products and personal and professional services. It appeals to businesses that prefer to be away from the dust and noise of the traffic in the streets. Today, Dymocks bookstore occupies three floors of the building, including street, mezzanine and lower ground levels, with an elegant café on the mezzanine floor. The café has become an iconic Sydney meeting point. Dymocks' head office occupies the sixth floor.

John Malcolm held the office of chairman until his death in 1963 at the age of 86. He led the company for more than 60 years – encompassing both World Wars and the Great Depression – and oversaw a period of almost continuous growth. He founded the New South Wales Booksellers Association and was co-founder of the Australian Booksellers Association, of which he was President from 1929 to 1949. John Malcolm was regarded as a shrewd businessman and invested heavily in property, including the historic Sydney Arcade, which he sold to G. J. Coles & Co. in 1950. Only the façade remains, at 97 King Street.

John Malcolm was succeeded as chairman by his son John William Hinton Forsyth. He had been working in his father's business for almost 40 years and already held the office of managing director. With his younger brother Malcolm he made significant changes to the way they operated the book arcade and the smaller store at Warringah Mall in the Sydney northern beaches suburb of Brookvale, opened on their father's watch. Cash and wrap counters operated 'supermarket style' and the number of staff was reduced to ensure that, according to Malcolm, 'only specialised people are available to assist customers, to point them in the direction of the books they want' (quoted in a 1974 *Sydney Morning Herald* article). Mail order and cash on delivery services, catalogues and costly special ordering services were discontinued. When John William Hinton died in 1976, having expanded the business, widened its range of books and opened up previously untapped sectors of the market, his brother Malcom took over the roles of chairman and managing director.

A revolution begins

In 1981 William Dymock's great nephew John Pemberton Curlewis Forsyth decided to sell his own successful printing and publishing business and buy the family company. Although

Dymocks was not in trouble it wasn't performing well. There was little resistance to the sale of shares to John from the family and preference shareholders.

John started his own business while he was still at school, duplicating documents for lawyers. It gradually grew into a lucrative printing company with about 270 staff and a magazine publishing division, with a stable of 40 magazines including the *Australian Stock Exchange Journal* and *Big League*.

Dymocks had two stores when John acquired the business, which included the book arcade that occupied the ground floor of the Dymocks building and the very small store at Warringah Mall. John planned to spend about $6 million on refurbishing the building as a landlord and was intending to ask the management to prepare the wholesale and retail bookselling business for sale. He says, 'But I got hooked on the bookselling business and decided against selling. Massive changes had to be made.'

John considered the whole book industry to be 'hopelessly old-fashioned'. He spent three months travelling overseas, searching for ideas, writing reports and taking photos. John recalls, 'I couldn't find anything exceptional except for one group of bookstores in Canada that were doing it in a different way. Everywhere else the bookstores were like libraries, spine out, dusty – like it was here.'

John returned ready to take Dymocks Book Arcade into a new and exciting era, with full computerisation, total refurbishment and a change of character. However, he had no expertise in retailing. He had been involved in the mining, printing and magazine publishing industries. Well aware of the risk of rebuilding a retailing business without experience, John put together a team of experts with impressive track records in marketing, shopfitting, retailing, merchandising and advertising to create an implementation plan.

Unfortunately, what works in theory doesn't necessarily work in practice. John explains:

> 'We traded through the refurbishment. It was a total disaster. We'd removed everything and started all over again, bringing it to what we thought would appeal to book buyers when it was up and running. Sales were down by one-third. We couldn't work it out, and after about three months we considered going back to "Plan A", which was to keep the building and sell the bookselling business. But none of us wanted to do it. We gave it another week, then another week, then another month. It was very expensive.'

After about seven months, book sales began to lift and it wasn't long before they were soaring at an increasing rate. Dymocks' market share increased dramatically. John explains:

> 'The only rationale for the turnaround was that at first, we were alienating existing customers who may have preferred a library feel, with books being displayed "spine out" and no strong merchandising. It appears that we attracted younger customers, who took some time to find us. In any case, it was very successful.'

In 1984, Dymocks purchased the Pocket and Technical Bookshop, relocated it, expanded it and staffed it with specialists in the technical, education, computer and literary fields. Dymocks developed its own computerised system with four in-store terminals and a database of some 120,000 titles. John recalls, 'We searched all over the world for a system that was designed with the customer in mind rather than the retailer. It became apparent that such a system didn't exist, so we had to create our own.'

The Pocket and Technical Bookshop, only 300 metres north of the Sydney flagship store, gave Dymocks two major outlets in the heart of Sydney. However, its customers preferred shopping at the flagship store, so the newly acquired store was closed at the end of the 15-year lease and became part of the flagship store.

A new model: franchising

Following the success of refitting the flagship store in George Street, Dymocks started to open more stores in New South Wales and reached a total of 12 before John recalled the advice of two of his printing and publishing clients who had worked for KFC and McDonald's. They had introduced him to the concept of franchising. John remembers, 'One thing I learnt was that a franchise would outperform a company-owned store by between 20% and 30% in terms of sales per square metre of space. It could also operate at lower cost. It's a winning formula for both the franchisee and the franchisor.' He adds, 'I knew all this while I was in the publishing and printing business, but I couldn't franchise that because of the cost of the huge printing machines.'

> A franchise would outperform a company-owned store by between 20% and 30% in terms of sales per square metre of space.

John set up a company store in Bondi in 1985, got it up and running well, put in his best store manager and pushed it as hard as he could. He then sold the business to a franchisee and watched as sales went up significantly and costs came down. John declares, 'I put it down to it being the franchisee's money on the line. But I still wasn't convinced.' He repurchased the store from the franchisee and resumed operating it with company staff. It traded profitably but didn't perform nearly as well as it had for the franchisee. In the final stage of John's experiment he sold the business to a new franchisee, thinking that, in his own words, 'Maybe we just lucked into a really super salesman the first time.' Sales went up again and costs came down.

Although the experiment was limited in extent, the Dymocks board was convinced that franchising was the best strategy for the long-term growth of the company. The Dymocks Franchise System was set up in 1985 and grew slowly and cautiously at first. At the end of 1987, there were only three franchised stores, all in suburban Sydney. Since then, Dymocks stores have been successfully opened throughout the country, with CBD flagship stores in every capital city. The Sydney, Perth and four other large stores are company-owned and the Brisbane store is a partnership with a franchisee. All other stores, about 60 of them, are franchised.

John Forsyth feels a great sense of satisfaction with the Dymocks Franchise System:

> 'We like it because the franchisees own and operate the business and tailor it to their local community. It is vitally important that both the franchisee and the franchisor earn a satisfactory return on their investment. The franchisees must make money or it's not viable. But they must conform with our formula and required standard of service. In return for a franchise fee and advertising fee, both of which are a percentage of sales, we provide all advertising, promotion, buying terms, commercial advice, brand awareness, and our reputation for excellence and integrity. The effect of this is to allow the franchisee access to the benefits of a large business that a small business could not contemplate.'

New directions

Even before Dymocks spread its wings to every state and territory it had ventured overseas. The first Dymocks store in New Zealand opened in 1994 and three years later Dymocks announced a 55% interest in a joint venture with the *South China Morning Post* to open Dymocks branded stores in Hong Kong. Three of the Hong Kong stores closed in 2012 and the remainder in 2015. According to John it was impossible to make the Hong Kong stores profitable because every two years the landlord required refurbishment in order to renew leases. The New Zealand stores were sold so that the company could focus on the Australian market, with the last store in Auckland closing in 2012.

Dymocks had been investing in property for many years, beginning with the purchase of the Royal Hotel building by John Malcolm Forsyth in 1922; it continues to invest today through the Dymocks Properties division. The property assets are valued at some hundreds of millions of dollars. One of its most significant purchases was the Guardian Assurance building on the corner of Sydney's Pitt and Hunter Streets in 1991. A 12-level office tower, it was fully leased by high-end tenants and represented a shrewd and high-yielding purchase. In 2014, Dymocks purchased a 16,000 square metre commercial office building in St Kilda Road, Melbourne. In 2019, it purchased a 6,000 square metre building in George Street, Brisbane, within the legal precinct and adjacent to the courts. The office building is occupied by more than 40 tenants mostly from within the legal profession. Dymocks has other properties in Brisbane, Western Australia and Tasmania.

In 2009, Dymocks purchased an 80% interest in Healthy Habits, a chain of franchised sandwich, salad and juice bars, with the intention of dramatically increasing the number of stores. With increasing competition and, according to John, the difficulty in finding franchisees who wanted to make sandwiches all day, the business was sold in 2016.

Dymocks made a much more successful acquisition in 2010 when it purchased Melbourne-based confectionery manufacturer Patons, specialists in chocolate-coated nut products. In 2012, Patons acquired the Suncoast Gold Macadamia retail brand and expanded its range of products further when it purchased the Gourmet Nut Company in 2015 and renamed itself as Patons Macadamia. Ann Verschuer, John's partner in life, with a horticulture background, oversees an 80,000-tree macadamia plantation and avocado crops as managing director of the Farming Division of the Dymocks Group.

The 80,000 macadamia tree plantation is located in Yarrahapinni on the mid-north coast of NSW.

Dymocks expanded further in 2015 when it acquired Telegram, a wholesaler and distributor of designer stationery, homeware and luxury brands including Lamy and Moleskine. Telegram's retail arm, Milligram, operates a thriving online store and opened its first bricks and mortar store at the Melbourne Central shopping centre in 2017. Since then, Milligram has opened stores at Doncaster, Highpoint and Carlton, all in Victoria. The stores are home to some of the world's classiest designer stationery, office and lifestyle accessories.

In late 2018, Dymocks ventured into education with the launch of Potentia tutoring centres in the Sydney suburbs of Parramatta and Bankstown. John explains, 'Potentia is not just "more school". It goes much further than just improving performance in exams.' The learning hubs and tuition have been designed by highly regarded academics, psychologists and counsellors. Potentia's teachers are chosen for their ability to build confidence and inspire enthusiasm for learning. Although Dymocks has no intention of expanding overseas in books, it will take its educational initiatives beyond Australian shores through Potentia.

Changing times

With the launch of Amazon in 1995, Australia's bookselling industry was about to be turned on its head. Australian bookstore Angus & Robertson launched its online store in the same year and others followed. This created a major challenge for all book retailers. Dymocks launched its online bookstore in 2006 in response to customer demand and it is now thriving, largely as a result of continual updates of technology, including artificial intelligence.

> Dymocks Booklovers are avid and frequent buyers and account for over 40% of all sales.

Dymocks launched an in-store loyalty program called Dymocks Booklover Rewards in 2001 which, like most of its counterparts, offered discounts and other incentives to engender customer loyalty. It was refreshed and relaunched online in 2006 to bring Dymocks much closer to its regular customers.

The Booklover program has undergone a series of upgrades and improvements since 2006 and, according to John, in recent years it has been largely responsible for sales growth well beyond that of the total book market. The program now boasts more than a million members across Australia. 'Dymocks Booklovers are avid and frequent buyers and account for over 40% of all sales,' says John. He adds, 'As well as loyalty encouragement it gets us much closer to our customers and allows us to provide them with information about upcoming literary events. We use analytics and artificial intelligence to find out what each customer loves to read and make helpful recommendations to them based on that.'

Turmoil hit the bookselling trade in 2011 when REDgroup, which operated two of Australia's largest retail chains, Borders and Angus & Robertson, went into voluntary liquidation, eventually forcing the closure of all of its stores. REDgroup, owned by a private equity company, had massive debt and sustained losses over several years. The crisis began in 2007 when Borders USA put its entire Australian and New Zealand operations on the market. Dymocks considered purchasing Borders and Angus & Robertson but decided to step back after assessing the businesses as unsustainable.

REDgroup owned Angus & Robertson and was already burdened with high levels of debt when it acquired Borders' Australasian stores in 2008. The demise of the group was attributed to debt, poor management and an inability to adapt to the online market. When it collapsed in 2011, it accounted for about 20% of the Australian book market, while Dymocks had about 11%. This left a gap that Dymocks was well able to help fill. Unlike REDgroup, Dymocks had little debt and had been able to successfully adapt to online retailing of books. It also offered a much more personal and positive level of in-store customer service. The impact of competition from discount department stores like Target, Kmart and Big W has changed little in recent years. Dymocks customers have remained loyal and appreciate the access to a much wider range of titles.

Engaging the community

Since the opening of its first store in 1879, Dymocks has actively supported a lifelong love of learning through reading in its community. The Dymocks of today sees literacy and community education as a priority. As a bookseller, the company is ideally placed to leverage its suppliers and encourage its staff and customers to support disadvantaged children, schools and communities.

Dymock's Literary Events Club arranges literary lunches and other events where local and international authors speak about their books and lives. The lunches are generally held in five-star hotels all around Australia and offer an opportunity for members and guests to be entertained and engaged by authors who may be novelists, biographers, actors, politicians, celebrities or just ordinary people with extraordinary stories to tell. Between 300 and 1,000 guests attend the lunches to enjoy a three-course meal while listening to a well-known author discuss his or her book.

Most Dymocks stores host a range of in-store events such as book launches, signings and readings, which are designed to engage the local community, particularly children, with authors and books.

Dymocks Children's Charities began in August 2000 as Dymocks Literacy Foundation with the purpose of helping children in need with literacy. 'Our vision is to change kids' lives – one book at a time!', says John. 'We provide programs in pre-schools and primary schools in underprivileged locations. We want to encourage kids to read every day just because they want to. Quite simply, it's about getting good books into kids' hands. Although our aims are relatively simple, the results can be life-changing, boosting a child's self-esteem and opportunities for a fulfilling future. We know that a child who reads for pleasure every day becomes a lifelong learner.'

> Our vision is to change kids' lives – one book at a time!

The charity holds a fundraising event in March or April each year called The Great Debate. 'Between 500 and 600 people enjoy a great evening of entertainment whilst bidding at live and silent auctions using smartphones to raise money for the various programs we deliver,' says Ann Verschuer. One of the charity's programs is the Book Bank, which gives children books of their choice. 'In a lot of instances these will be the first books they have ever owned,' says John.

Reflections

Looking back over the past 140 years, John is deeply proud of his family, past and present. 'We've always managed to stay afloat in the hard times, such as the World Wars, the Great Depression, the recession of the 1990s and the GFC.' He admits that there have been errors of judgement. 'It was unfortunate that the building was constructed before the depression. It must have turned my grandfather grey.'

The expansion into Hong Kong and New Zealand, along with the purchase of Healthy Habits, clearly didn't work – but on the other hand, there were lessons to be learnt from those experiences. John reflects on them, refusing to see them as setbacks:

'We really don't believe in setbacks, we don't believe in
problems, we believe in opportunities. You can always
find an opportunity in a problem. For example, the sale
of Healthy Habits provided the opportunity to purchase
Telegram.'

There is no doubt that the introduction of franchising provided a springboard for further growth, but John asserts: 'The business would have stayed afloat without franchising but would have grown much more slowly.' Each franchise store is a small business in its own right and the franchisees are highly motivated. John believes that ownership drives performance and sales figures certainly support his contention.

According to John, the franchisees and their staff know their customers and talk to them about what they are reading. 'It's a personal approach, which you won't find in the big discount stores, and our customers really appreciate that. The franchise model positions us very well for the future in bookselling and can be adapted for new ventures.'

Interior of the modern Dymocks store in the Highpoint shopping centre, Melbourne.

The online store has had less impact on the number of customers visiting real stores than the company expected. 'Many of them go online to search for a book and then go to the store to buy it,' says John. It seems that for book enthusiasts, nothing beats walking through a bookstore and browsing, chatting to knowledgeable staff and finding an unexpected treasure on the shelves.

Ann Verschuer describes John Forsyth as 'a person who sees opportunities that other people don't see and acts on them. He is a "now and future guy", with little interest in the past.' It was John who turned an underperforming Dymocks around when he sold his own successful business and bought out all other shareholders. John adds, 'Ann and I make a strong team and highly value each other's opinion.' Teamwork is an important factor in the success of the business and is evident at all levels.

Differences of opinion are openly discussed at board level and employees recognise that they are part of the team; a high proportion remain with the company for many years. According to John, being recognised as National Book Retailer of the Year at the Australian Book Industry Awards in 2015, 2016 and 2018 demonstrates the value of teamwork in running the company and within each store, whether company-owned or franchised.

John Pemberton Curlewis Forsyth AM

Owner and chairman of Dymocks since 1981, John Forsyth has every right to be proud of his achievements. Yet he is a modest man, quick to acknowledge the role played by his partner Ann, his family and his employees in the success of the Dymocks Group.

John has always been interested in aviation and both he and Ann are licensed helicopter pilots. He was appointed Chairman of Air Services Australia in 1996, an office which he held for eight years. He was honoured as a Member of the Order of Australia (AM) in 2005 'for philanthropy and service to aviation as an adviser to government and as a leader in the development and automation of air traffic systems in Australia.'

John expresses great pride in the integrity of the Dymocks Group and the Dymocks Building, which the company gives high priority to maintaining in pristine condition. 'We regard our greatest asset as integrity. It takes a long time to build it but you can destroy it overnight,' he says with great conviction.

John is especially proud of Dymocks Children's Charities and the role it plays in improving the lives of children.

Until the 1980s, the women in the Forsyth family took no active role in the business. John Forsyth's late wife Marion had a role as a director and his partner Ann, as well as managing the macadamia and avocado plantations, is a director, mentor and adviser, with a key role in strategic planning. Ann was appointed to the board in February 2001. Marion was instrumental firstly in Dymocks' support of Spine Care, a charity dealing with spinal injury, and subsequently the formation of what is now Dymocks Children's Charities. John observes, 'Women have become progressively more influential and stronger in society and this has been reflected in the business.' He believes that the role of women will continue to grow and, as an aside, proposes, 'The world would be a better place if it were run by women. Not so much testosterone and ego.'

Moving forward

John believes that the business will remain in family hands for many years to come. Although there is no formal family succession plan in place, he believes that his son John Ferguson Dymock Forsyth is likely to succeed him as chairman of the Dymocks Group. John Ferguson has a keen interest in aviation, is a partner in a successful business in Portland, Oregon and is also a partner in a heavy-lift helicopter business in Indonesia, in which Dymocks has a 50% interest. However, there is no guarantee that the younger John will lead the business. As the older John explains:

> 'My first and foremost business advice to my children was to look for something they love and work out how to make a living from it. If you love doing something you usually do it extremely well. They may remain as owners and may be directors, but they should feel no obligation to come into the business. Our succession plan is to ensure that we continually attract the best professional managers and talent into the business at every level.'

In the event of the inability or lack of interest of a family member to step up into senior management, John Pemberton Curlewis Forsyth has ensured that there are competent, professional and experienced people within the company to keep it flourishing. John explains:

'Each business in the group has its own extremely competent managing director, selected on merit. Each MD must be passionate about the business and treat it as their own. As chairman, I have to let them make mistakes. I can't breathe down their neck. They need to be able to do things their way. That's one of the most important things for a family-owned company. If you exert too much control and you drop dead, it tends to fall apart.'

The Dymocks Group of Companies now includes Dymocks Booksellers, Dymocks Properties, Dymocks Children's Charities, Patons Macadamia, Telegram, Milligram, Arapala, which is a sizable macadamia and avocado plantation, and Potentia Education. As chairman of the Dymocks Group, John aims to ensure that the business continues to reinvent itself in response to the ever-changing Australian market, while at the same time preserving its heritage and integrity.

Dymocks Bookstores, the oldest but not the largest segment of the business, continues to be well ahead of its competitors. John says, 'Our innovations in store design, online presence and marketing have been continuous.' One of the latest innovations is the introduction of kiosks to the larger Dymocks stores. The kiosks allow customers to use a touchscreen to search for specific titles, browse by category, scroll through a store map or even get recommendations based on their interests, all fed from the Dymocks website artificial intelligence recommendations system. The buying and merchandising teams can view and report on the searches and browsing flow of customers, allowing them to identify the most sought-after products – even before they start selling.

Despite the commonly held belief that there is not much of a future for traditional books, the reality is different. According to Ann Verschuer, books have had a revival. 'We've noticed that e-books are in decline around the world and believe that people get more pleasure from reading that is not associated with computers and devices related to their work,' says Ann. 'As new technology continues to roll out, Dymocks must make a broader offering of books, associated products and education-related products to its customers,' she reflects, predicting, 'The Dymocks store of the future will look very different from the stores of today.'

CHAPTER 5

BROWN FAMILY WINE GROUP

NOT A BAD DROP

Photo on previous page shows John Charles Brown with his four sons in the winery. From left: Ross, Roger, John Charles, Peter and John Graham.

RENOWNED FOR THE DIVERSITY of its wine varieties and styles, Brown Brothers has been one of the most successful family-owned wine companies in Australia for more than 130 years. Since the planting of its very first vineyard near the small town of Milawa in Victoria's King Valley in 1885, the Brown family's affinity for adventure and experimentation has led to the development of an expansive range of wines and some completely new grape varieties.

Today, the third and fourth generation of Brown family winemakers are keeping the tradition of innovative and passionate winemaking alive, with vineyards in four locations across Victoria and another two in Tasmania. The climatic conditions of the Brown family's vineyards are as varied as its wine styles, ranging from cool alpine areas to lush temperate valleys to sun-drenched plains.

In recent years, Brown Brothers has transformed itself from a single brand to a family of brands, which includes Brown Brothers, Devil's Corner, Tamar Ridge, Pirie and Innocent Bystander. In September 2018, in recognition of the multiplicity of brands and the lack of brothers in the fourth generation, the company renamed itself the Brown Family Wine Group.

Starting small

The Milawa property that was to become the heart of Brown Brothers was purchased at a land auction in 1857 by Scottish-born John Graham. He established an orchard and small vineyard on the property. The scene was set for the establishment of Brown Brothers when George Harry Brown married John Graham's daughter Rebecca in 1864. George Brown was a Scottish migrant who had turned to farming after failing to make his fortune in the goldfields. When John Graham died in 1873 the Milawa property was transferred to George and Rebecca Brown.

In 1885, George's ambitious and imaginative 18-year-old son, John Francis Brown, talked his father into a partnership and they planted 10 acres of vines of mostly Riesling, Muscat and Shiraz on the property. Most of the property was still used to grow fruit and grain, which they sold by the roadside to gold miners travelling to and from the nearby town of Beechworth.

John Francis had absolutely no experience in winemaking, but he did have a burning ambition to succeed on the land. He was aware of the success of nearby Rutherglen as a wine-producing district and was convinced that the land in the King Valley was more suited to vineyards than grazing or cereal crops.

The hay and grain in the barn built by John Graham was cleared out and in 1889 it was used as a winery for the production of the first vintage at Milawa.

The Canadian Barn

John Graham initially migrated to Canada with his parents before sailing to Australia with his own young family. He built the barn on his Milawa property in the style of those that he was familiar with in Canada, for the storage of hay and grain. The steep pitch of the roof is designed to prevent the build-up of snow during the freezing Canadian winters – not in any way necessary at Milawa, which has probably experienced less than a couple of centimetres of snow in the 150 or so years since the barn was built.

The barn still stands today and has become known as the Canadian Barn. After falling into disrepair, it was completely restored in 2016 and is now used for weddings, other functions and company events and meetings.

During the depression of the 1890s, other winemakers in the district began going out of business. However, with a combination of business acumen, ingenuity and determination, John Francis was able to not only save his winery and vineyards from failure, but to expand them. By the end of 1896, he had bought out his father's share of the partnership and had planted a further 10 acres to vines. He named the vineyard Brown Bros in the hope that his three brothers would join him, but they had other interests and never did. In 1898, John Francis built a new weatherboard winery and cellar and was able to purchase some much sought after hand-crafted oak barrels and other equipment from wineries that had been forced to sell up. Four years later, he added a brick distillery for the production of fortifying spirit, which was used to make Muscat and Port.

Business was booming – so much so that in 1916 John Francis was able to purchase his own Model T Ford, at a time when any sort of automobile was a rare sight in rural Victoria. In that same year, the dreaded phylloxera, which had already devastated vineyards in other parts of Victoria, came to Milawa. This tiny insect destroys grapevines by feeding on their roots, causing the death of infested vines within six years. Over the following four years, John Francis ripped up his beloved vineyard, found a suitable "clean" site elsewhere on the property and, following the advice of Victorian government viticulturist François de Castella, ordered enough phylloxera-resistant rootstock to replant 35 acres. To the dismay of other winegrowers in the area, John Francis grafted varieties suited for table wines rather than the fortified wines favoured by most Australian wine consumers. Among the newly planted varieties were Riesling, Shiraz, Semillon and Cabernet Sauvignon.

John Francis was as energetic as he was ambitious. He was active in the local community throughout his life, serving as Shire Secretary and Treasurer of the Shire of Oxley, Honorary Secretary of the Free Library, Secretary of the Cemetery Trust and several other community organisations. During each of the two World Wars he served as Treasurer of the Milawa and District Patriotic Society. John Francis also served as President of the Rutherglen Wine Growers' Association.

In 1899, John Francis married Ida Peady and together they had four children, Bertha, Clarice, Ida and John Charles. As the only son, John Charles Brown was destined to take Brown Bros (again without brothers) into its second generation. John Charles completed his secondary education as a boarder at Scotch College in Melbourne and returned home to Milawa at the end of 1933. He was immediately set to work by his father. The winery was "buzzing" with a massive order of Tawny Port from London and a growing market for table wines among the newly arrived Italian migrants in the nearby Ovens Valley.

Ups and downs

Over the following 10 years, the softly spoken and quietly ambitious John Charles took on a succession of roles including delivery man, farm hand, accountant, salesman, vigneron and winemaker. In 1934, amid the Great Depression, he persuaded his father to open a cellar door, to allow people to come to taste and buy wine on the premises. The cost of transporting wine and dealing through distributors was becoming prohibitive and John Charles thought that a cellar door would attract customers to the winery, reducing its dependence on external sales.

The success of the cellar door was well beyond expectations, largely because of the growing population of Italian migrants in north eastern Victoria and their preference for table wines over fortified wines. Sales increased so much that Brown Bros had to double the size of its vineyard and purchase grapes from other growers. New varieties, including Grenache, White Grenache, White Hermitage and Palomino, were planted at Milawa.

By the time founder John Francis passed away in 1943 at the age of 76, John Charles had been effectively managing the vineyard and farm for several years. From the late 1930s, John Charles had faced some setbacks that tested his determination and could have stopped a lesser man in his tracks. A plague of grasshoppers completely destroyed the 1938 vintage, which had already been ravaged by a two-year drought. Following the outbreak of World War II, many of the regular pickers enlisted and there was a shortage of labour. In addition, during the war, interstate sales of all liquor was prohibited. For wineries like Brown Bros, situated not far from the New South Wales border, this ban caused a significant downturn in sales. To make matters worse, in 1943 another drought set in.

An enduring partnership

John Charles married Patricia Mathews in 1939, forming what was to become one of the most enduring and influential partnerships the Australian wine industry has seen. Initially, Patricia took no direct role in the family business because she was running the household and was busily engaged raising the couple's four sons, John Graham, Peter, Ross and Roger. There were always visitors and they were hosted around the family kitchen table. 'Mum had a natural flair for making simple food taste great and most of the ingredients came from the home garden,' Ross recalls. 'She also milked at least two cows every morning and evening. That's what you did on a family farm post-depression.'

As the boys were growing up, the conversation around the dinner table, dominated by the subjects of vineyards and wine varieties, inspired in Patricia what she called a 'slowly developing interest' in wine. Patricia's interest grew into a passion and she took pleasure in matching wine with food. In later years, she joined forces with her daughters-in-law, Judy and Jan, to provide regular catering for the expanding cellar door. John Graham recalls:

> 'As kids, there was always a glass of wine on the table for us and we were required to taste it, comment on the flavours we experienced and talk about its history and background.'

John Charles had learnt winemaking from his father and, like his father, he had a good business sense and was prepared to follow the technical advice of François de Castella. He was an innovator – even more progressive than his father. John Charles experimented with uncommon grape varieties and derived great pleasure from seeing so many well accepted by consumers. His innovations provided inspiration for the next generation.

In 1950, Brown Bros purchased the 117-acre Everton Hills property to the north east of Milawa. More elevated than the Milawa property, cooler and free of frost in winter, it was already planted with orchards and a small vineyard. One-third of the property was cleared and planted to bring the total area of vines, mostly Cabernet Sauvignon and Shiraz, to about 30 acres. Yields were low due to poor soil and low rainfall, but the quality of the grapes enabled the production of wines of great richness, depth and ageing potential.

At that time, sacrificing yield for high quality wine was not understood by consumers, who preferred less expensive wine from the higher yielding irrigation districts. The Everton Hills vineyard was unprofitable and eventually sold in 1977. Ross recalls that whenever the topic of selling the vineyard was raised, John Charles would host a barbeque on a hill overlooking the vines at the property, open a few old vintages and say, 'How could you sell this, the wine is so good.'

> How could you sell this, the wine is so good.

With a string of good vintages in the 1950s, and increasing demand for table wines by consumers, Brown Bros continued to expand and took advantage of newly emerging technology. The business started automating processes in 1961, replacing the hand grape presses with a hydraulic press. Refrigeration was installed in the same year, which rendered unnecessary the regular and tedious trips to the Wangaratta ice works to buy blocks of ice. Before refrigeration became available, the young fermenting juice was pumped through ice to reduce fermentation temperatures. Commercial refrigeration allowed John Charles to expand production, improve quality and develop new aromatic wine styles.

John Graham Brown, the eldest son of John Charles and Patricia, joined the family business in 1958 at the age of 17. Educated locally at first and then at Scotch College in Melbourne, just as his father was, there was never any doubt that John Graham would become a Brown Bros third-generation winemaker. He had spent most school holidays driving tractors in the vineyard, pumping wine, pressing grapes, washing vats and generally helping out in the winemaking process. He recalls:

'When I first went to primary school, I'd already decided that I wanted to be a winemaker.'

Four brothers working together

In 1965, John Graham married local schoolteacher June Ellis and, soon after the birth of his son John Andrew three years later, he assumed the role of chief winemaker from his father. He followed in his father's footsteps, experimenting with new grape varieties and innovative winemaking techniques. John Graham's three younger brothers, Peter, Ross and Roger, also educated locally and then at Scotch College, had never doubted that they would do anything else but work in the wine industry.

Peter Brown had always enjoyed his holiday work in the vineyards and even as a youngster he was fascinated with different grape varieties and viticultural experimentation. He joined the family business as vineyard manager at Milawa in 1963 after completing his secondary education. Peter also had a passion for all things mechanical and later developed an on-site mechanical maintenance workshop and welding shop, which provides services for the entire company.

Ross Brown followed his older brothers into the family business in 1966 at the age of 18 as manager of the cellar door. Since then he has overseen what has become one of Australia's most successful cellar doors, initiated and developed the Milawa Epicurean Centre and successfully steered Brown Bros wines into export markets throughout the world. Ross was also instrumental in encouraging investors to build a hotel on land that was annexed for them so that it would be close to the cellar door and Epicurean Centre.

Roger Brown, the youngest son of John Charles and Patricia Brown, always wanted to work in the vineyard. Unlike his older brothers, he didn't join the family business immediately after completing school. Instead, he worked in a Melbourne plant nursery for a year, learning simple nursery techniques that he would later apply in the family vineyards. He spent the following year in California and worked in a nursery which specialised in vine grafting. When Roger returned from California in 1976, he set up his own propagation farm, preparing for new plantings at Brown Bros' vineyards. Roger, like his older brother Peter, had remarkable mechanical skills and a passion for taking motorbikes apart, rebuilding them and riding them.

According to John Graham, his father was a "laissez-faire" style of leader:

> 'He gave the four of us the freedom to do our own thing. We each had different interests and didn't get under each other's feet. I was the winemaker, Peter was the outdoor type and loved the vineyards, Ross has the gift of the gab and is a natural at marketing and Roger took on the nursery role. He loved machinery, motor bikes and cars. He did some contract harvesting when mechanical harvesters became available.'

Not a bad drop!

John Charles Brown accepted praise of wines with great humility and his response to winning trophies and awards was invariably, 'not a bad drop'. The great Keith Dunstan wrote a book about Brown Brothers in 1999 and called it *Not a bad drop*. Keith says in the Introduction of the book, 'He must have said it a thousand times… It was a self put-down and it gave nothing away.' He added, '… it could have been the astounding 1962 Noble Riesling, the very wine that so many mistook for a Chateau d'Yquem. After receiving the praise he just smiled, *"not a bad drop"*.'

Expansion and innovation

The 1968 Milawa vintage was totally destroyed by a severe frost that devastated the vineyard in late 1967. The family subsequently purchased its frost-free 80-acre Mystic Park property in the Murray Valley to the north west. It was undeveloped and in a sorry state, but Peter Brown left Milawa and planted Mystic Park with numerous varieties suited to its soil and climate. The Mystic Park vineyard has since expanded to more than four times its original size.

With a number of vineyards exposed to a range of soils and climates, the potential for varietal diversity was exciting. In European terms, the diversity of vineyards could well be described "as cold as Champagne at one end and as hot as Sicily at the other".

Also, in response to the frost of 1967, Brown Bros drilled a bore at Milawa, hoping to find underground water. Not only did they find water, but it was of a high enough quality to use for drinking, washing and cleaning the equipment in the winery. It allowed them to defend against frost by installing overhead sprinklers to spray the vines with the tepid bore water and led to the development of an irrigation system that negated the effect of droughts, protected the vineyard from frost and provided a new sense of certainty.

Had it not been for that disastrous frost and seeing a similar frost protection system in California, they would never have searched for underground water and there would have been no bore. Since it was drilled, the water supply at Milawa has been reliable and production has increased. John Graham reflects, 'We've had our fair share of setbacks, but each setback has resulted in a giant step forward.'

> We've had our fair share of setbacks, but each setback has resulted in a giant step forward.

The discovery of underground water, along with further investment in new technology for the winery, was followed by a succession of excellent vintages. The "dream run" was interrupted in 1977 by a mini cyclone and hailstorm that almost destroyed the winery and all but wiped out the vintage from the Milawa vineyard.

Brown Bros' network of vineyards continued to grow with the establishment in 1974 of the Hurdle Creek vineyard, only a few kilometres from Milawa. The business purchased the St Leonards winery at Wahgunyah in north east Victoria in 1980. In 1982, the Whitlands vineyard, 800 metres above the King Valley, was purchased and planted to varieties suited to the cooler climate, including Riesling, Pinot Noir, Chardonnay and Merlot. Roger was instrumental in providing new vines for the growing collection of vineyards. At Milawa the cellar door was redeveloped and expanded.

With four brothers now in the business, Brown Bros became Brown Brothers; the change appeared on wine labels from 1980.

In 1985, Roger Brown was diagnosed with a brain tumour. He later underwent surgery which kept the tumour at bay for three years, but tragically lost his battle in 1990. Roger is survived by his wife Elu and daughters Stephanie and Phillipa.

In 1988, John Charles, aged 73, stepped down as managing director of Brown Brothers and took on the role of chairman.

John Graham relinquished his role of chief winemaker to take his father's place. In turn, for the first time a chief winemaker was appointed from outside the family.

John Charles Brown AM

John Charles Brown was widely acknowledged as one of Australia's foremost winemaking innovators. He was much loved and admired in the wine industry and generous with his support of new entrants to the industry. His efforts were acknowledged in 1989 when he was appointed as a Member of the Order of Australia (AM) for services to the wine industry.

John Charles was further honoured in 2003 with a Restaurant & Catering Australia Lifetime Achievement Award, in recognition of his outstanding achievements as a pioneering winemaker, developer of regional tourism and supporter of the broader industry.

The innovations roll on

The expansion and innovation at Brown Brothers continued at a rapid pace under the leadership of John Charles' son John Graham Brown. At the forefront of his innovations is the Kindergarten Winery, a miniature winery designed as a research and development facility. Established in 1989, the Kindergarten Winery allows the winemaking team to experiment with new grape varieties and wine styles in small quantities and experiment with different viticultural and winemaking practices. The new wines produced in the Kindergarten Winery are trialled at the cellar door. If they prove popular, their production is moved out of the Kindergarten Winery so that larger batches can be made. Some of the experimental grape varieties developed in the Kindergarten Winery, including Cienna, Tempranillo, Pinot Grigio, Moscato and Prosecco, have since become widely available and popular.

The Kindergarten Winery, which was designed by John Graham Brown's son John Andrew.

In 1990, Brown Brothers created a Viticultural Research and Development team, extending its pioneering work from the winery to the vineyards. This created the perfect product development cycle, from growing, making, trialling in the Kindergarten to marketing through the cellar door. Through this dynamic process, Brown Brothers continues to lead the industry with new wine styles and varietal flavours.

The year 1994 was very special for Brown Brothers on a number of fronts. John Charles celebrated his 60th vintage and his grandson John Andrew (son of John Graham) joined the company – the fourth generation of family winemakers. The Milawa Epicurean Centre, a restaurant dedicated to matching delightful food with the flavours and complexities of Brown Brothers wines, was opened. The business purchased Banksdale Vineyard, with an elevation of 450 metres, in the western King Valley, adding to the diversity of vineyards and providing an ideal site for many of the classic Italian varieties including Prosecco.

In 1998, Brown Brothers added further to its diverse range of vineyards with the purchase and development of 500 acres of land in the Heathcote wine region of Central Victoria. The Heathcote region, slightly warmer and drier, than the King Valley, is well known for its red soils and rich spicy Shiraz. This vineyard has become the company's main source of fruit for the classic red varieties Shiraz, Cabernet and Merlot. Further plantings of new varieties included richly-flavoured Tempranillo, Durif and Petit Verdot as single vineyard wines.

The new millennium brought with it a number of major changes at Brown Brothers. In 2001, at the age of 69, John Graham relinquished his role as chief executive to pursue other interests that a seven-day-a-week job didn't allow. John and June love the outback and have visited virtually every significant site and outback track across the deserts of Australia. He continued his active involvement in the family business as chairman of the board until he stepped down in favour of non-executive chairman Sandy Clark in 2007. John's younger brother Ross was subsequently appointed as the new chief executive. Being conscious of the need for a smooth transition between generations, in 2010 John Graham encouraged his son John Andrew to take on his role on the board. In the following year, Ross resigned as chief executive, so that he could concentrate on strategic development as executive director. His replacement was former winemaker and general manager Roland Wahlquist. These changes marked the beginning of a new era of governance at Brown Brothers, with

Patricia and John Charles Brown.

a more independent board who had a greater depth of business experience.

The man often hailed as the father of the Victorian wine industry, John Charles Brown, passed away in May 2004 at the age of 89 as his 70th vintage at Milawa was drawing to a close. His wife Patricia passed away only four months later. With the enthusiastic support of Patricia and his four sons, John Charles had established Brown Brothers as the most visited winery in Australia.

At his father's funeral ceremony, held in a packed Epicurean Centre, John Graham spoke about a wonderful lesson delivered to him by his father:

> 'One day, not long after leaving school, Dad and I were working in the cellar when Dad made the comment, "You four boys can really make something out of this place, but only if you all work together." He had a vine cutting in his hand, which he broke in half, saying, "See how easily it's broken when there is only one?" He then put the pieces together, saying, "See how much harder they are to break when there are two?" He then put four pieces together, saying, "See… now it's almost impossible to break them. This is the strength you and your brothers can have if you work together."'

The first release of the Patricia range was in 2003. The current range of Patricia wines comprises Pinot Noir and Chardonnay Brut, Chardonnay, Shiraz, Cabernet Sauvignon and Noble Riesling. Only the very best fruit of each variety are used to craft the Patricia range. As the wines are made in limited quantities, they are all produced in the Kindergarten Winery.

Ross Brown recalls, 'When I told my mother that we were planning to release a premium range in her honour she replied, "They had better be bloody good."'

Mum's the word

The flagship Patricia range of wines has been named in recognition of Patricia Brown's passion for the family business and for the love and inspiration that she gave her family. During the years of enormous growth in the 1970s and 1980s, the family's daily routine was to meet at the family dining table at 10.30am to discuss the business.

Patricia, known by all as Pat, was the tea lady and the person who heard all the discussions. If there was a debate about the business, the wine or food, Pat usually had the last call and was not to be messed with. Ross Brown's wife Judy recalls that Patricia would never extend an invitation to the daughters-in-law to morning tea. She even heated the tea cups to extend the length of the discussion. This daily communication, with all the stakeholders around the table, might well be the reason for the longevity and success of Brown Brothers.

In June 2005, John Graham Brown was appointed as an Officer in the Order of Australia (AO) for services to the wine industry and the promotion of rural and regional economic development initiatives in Victoria and to the community through his service to the Country Fire Authority.

In November 2005, the Brown family was rocked by another tragedy when Peter Brown was killed in a motorcycle accident at the age of 60. Peter had managed the St Leonards Vineyard and the All Saints Vineyard, both in the Rutherglen wine region, since they were purchased by Brown Brothers in 1980 and 1992 respectively. He purchased both of them from the family as his own in 1999.

In 2010, Brown Brothers acquired two vineyards in Tasmania along with the Devil's Corner, Tamar Ridge and Pirie wineries. The acquisition was largely driven by Ross Brown's determination to find the best locations to grow the cool climate variety

Pinot Noir. He was also influenced by climate change and the increasing frequency of drought, bushfires and frosts. 'We wanted to futureproof our business. If there are destructive weather events in Victoria, we can compensate for it elsewhere,' he says. 'Dad's fascination with trout fishing in Tasmania may have been another factor in the choice of new location,' says his daughter Caroline.

Generation four

The four Brown brothers had two sons and eight daughters between them. There was no guarantee that any of them would join the business but today there are three fourth-generation members of the family working full-time in the business and another two are non-executive directors.

John Andrew Brown, only son of John Graham and June Brown, joined the family business in 1994 after working at BHP as an engineer, where he gained invaluable experience in project management. His first task at Brown Brothers was to develop a computer-based management information system that took the company to the forefront of business systems and the information age. John also spent time in the winery and won a trophy for one of his fortified wines. John is currently pursuing interests outside the business.

John Andrew's sister Cynthia worked in human resources before joining the family business in time for the 1996 vintage, gaining first-hand experience in winemaking. She then worked in the cellar door and in the Epicurean Centre before being appointed as direct marketing manager in 1998. Three years later, Cynthia was appointed as employment services manager, taking responsibility for recruitment and performance management across the company. She resigned in 2005 to pursue business interests outside the company but sits on the board as a non-executive director.

Peter Brown's children Eliza, Angela and Nicholas, all work at their independently owned All Saints Estate, St Leonards Vineyard and Mount Ophir Estate in Victoria's Rutherglen wine region. Eliza is chief executive officer of the three businesses. As sales and marketing director, Angela oversees all elements of growing brands, local sales, exports, marketing and public relations. Nicholas completed a Bachelor of Oenology degree at the University of Adelaide in 2006. As general manager of the businesses, he heads the winemaking and viticulture team and manages all vineyards. All three are shareholders in the Brown Family Wine Group. Eliza was elected to the Brown Brothers board after the death her father in 2005 and remains a member of the board of the Brown Family Wine Group.

Ross and Judy Brown have three daughters, Katherine, Caroline and Emma. All three are passionate about the family business. Katherine Brown has a Master's degrees in Wine Business and Oenology and Viticulture. After gaining experience in Bordeaux and Champagne, she joined the business as public relations manager and brand manager. Katherine joined the winemaking team in 2015, becoming the first female winemaker in the family. She also serves on the Victorian Government Wine Ministerial Advisory Committee. Caroline and Emma have both completed Bachelor of Communications (Business) degrees at Bond University. Caroline has worked her way up to the position of public relations and corporate communications manager. Emma worked for Treasury Wine Estates in the Napa Valley, managing the Penfolds brand, before joining the business and is now marketing manager of the Brown Family Wine Group.

Reflections

Throughout its history, innovation has remained at the core of the Brown family business. It began with founder, John Francis Brown, planting grape varieties not previously thought to be suitable for the King Valley or Australian tastes. The rate of innovation accelerated under the leadership of his son John Charles and grandson John Graham, who experimented with uncommon varieties, built the Kindergarten Winery and collaborated with the CSIRO to develop completely new grape varieties able to use less water, grow in warmer climates and tolerate different types of soil. Today, the current team of winemakers, including Katherine, have taken on the mantle of innovation.

The biggest success story of the CSIRO collaboration is Cienna, first planted as A871, which produces a slightly sweeter style of red wine with a lower alcohol content than traditional reds. Created in 1972, and first released to the public in 2000, Cienna is now Brown Brothers' top selling red wine. The collaboration with the CSIRO continues, with several unnamed varieties in tanks in the Kindergarten Winery.

The Milawa Epicurean Centre, which opened in 1994, was also an innovation. While cellar doors throughout Australia were beginning to offer food as well as tasting, Brown Brothers was the first to open a restaurant dedicated to matching wine with gourmet food.

John Graham is proud of the esteem in which the Brown Brothers brand is held and the way the company has grown. He recalls that when he joined the company in 1958 he was one of only six staff. Now the Brown Family Wine Group employs more than 200 full-time staff and the brand name is increasingly recognised in Australia and throughout the world. He would like to see the company continuing to grow and to be known as one of the best family wine companies in the world and renowned for quality, consistency and good value for money.

Throughout its history, Brown Brothers has been actively involved in the community and wine industry organisations. It was one of 12 foundation members of Australia's First Families of Wine (AFFW), established in 2009 to create an awareness of the quality and regional diversity of Australian premium wines in export markets. The collective includes other family-owned wine companies including Yalumba, McWilliams and Henschke. Ross explains, 'As a group we have a much stronger voice internationally.'

While AFFW has been successful in achieving its primary aim, the strength of the relationships formed between members of the next generation has been an unexpected outcome. Ross says:

> 'Through AFFW, the sons and daughters of each of the member families have found that they have common interests. They've found out that they are not the only people who work hard and think that the wine business is the greatest business in the world. They are more engaged in the business than they would have been without AFFW and each family benefits by having a next generation that is more likely to perpetuate their business.'

In the broader community, the Brown Family Wine Group has a social responsibility strategy, which encapsulates sustainability within the environment, the communities that the business impacts upon and its employees at all levels. Although the group has access to huge underground reserves of water at Milawa, along with sufficient rainfall in the nearby hills, it is very conscious of the need to reduce its use of water. Subsurface irrigation in vineyards located in drier regions allows water to trickle under the vines, reducing weeds and the need for herbicides and cutting water use dramatically. Soil moisture monitoring technology and weather stations across all vineyard sites aid in accurate irrigation scheduling. Vineyard mulching programs reduce water use even further and improve soil structure.

In addition to these measures, the Brown Family Wine Group is always working on improving energy efficiency. 'A state-of-the-art warehouse at Milawa has no mechanical refrigeration. The walls and roof are heavily insulated and we maintain a temperature of less than 20 degrees Celsius by using fans that draw in cool air at night,' explains John Graham. 'We've also reduced our use of tractors in the vineyard and have a carbon-reduction team looking for more ways of reducing our carbon footprint.' Among other measures are more sustainable packaging and increased recycling.

Although Brown Brothers wines have won numerous trophies and medals, Ross Brown maintains that producing Australia's top selling Moscato and Prosecco is much more important than winning awards. 'For a number of years in a row we were voted Australia's consumers' most loved Australian wine brand,' says Ross. 'These successes are recognition that we are achieving one of our most important goals, which is to be loved by our customers. But above all, our desire is to remain a sustainable and successful family-owned company for generations to come.'

> Above all, our desire is to remain a sustainable and successful family-owned company for generations to come.

Ross Brown's greatest source of pride is the acquisition of Tasmanian vineyards and brands. 'Taking the big step to Tasmania has been a great triumph, especially as we took some big risks to do it,' he says. 'We took on industry leadership on climate change by moving to a cooler climate when it was only just being discussed. Now everyone wants to be in Tasmania and Brand Tasmania's turned out to be a bit of a gem for us as well.' Daughter Caroline cites surviving over 130 years and the successful transition into the next generation as her greatest source of pride.

The Brown Family Wine Group and its brands are internationally recognised. Although Brown Brothers began exporting their wine during the 1930s and again in the 1970s, mainly to New Zealand, exports didn't really become significant until after the Australian dollar was floated in 1983. Its value dropped and all Australian exports became significantly cheaper.

The group currently exports to 20 countries including China, New Zealand, South Korea, Singapore, Germany, Sweden and the Netherlands. The growth of the Chinese market in the last 10 years has ignited strong interest. Caroline Brown says:

'China has been incredibly strong for us. While everyone else was exporting Shiraz, we looked at what people like to drink and found that Chinese consumers enjoy fruitier and sweeter wines, so we took our Moscato and the slightly sweet and fruity red Cienna and they're both doing really well.'

Moving forward

After more than 130 years, four generations and a history of innovation, ingenuity and determination, the Brown Family Wine Group has a succession plan in place to ensure that the company remains strong and in family hands. A code of practice defines the employment conditions for family members, which includes a requirement that after completing their education they work for four years elsewhere before applying for a position in the company.

'There is no sense of entitlement,' says fourth-generation Caroline. 'We have to be qualified for the role we undertake.' Her uncle John Graham agrees, pointing out that family members are employed on merit. 'We want to ensure that family members don't take someone else's job just because they're a Brown,' he says. His brother Ross adds, 'To be a globally successful business you have to have the best person for each role, and that applies all the way up to board level.'

Ross reflects:

'You have to be pragmatic today. If a multi-generational family business isn't thriving and giving you a return on investment, the shareholders – all members of the family – are going to get pretty upset. You have to deliver and keep on delivering. The process of succession planning is never finished. You can't just lock it away, it's a continuous journey.'

One of the primary reasons for the ongoing success of Brown Brothers and now the Brown Family Wine Group has been its ability to adapt to changes in the wine industry, which has required the appointment of highly skilled specialists from outside the family to winemaking roles and senior management and the board. The six-member board includes three non-family members, one of whom is chairman.

Ross is optimistic about the future of the business, saying:

'It has been our shared vision that has achieved the sustained drive and energy over more than 130 years. We have worked really well and harmoniously as a family supported by sensational staff. We have seen the business go from a family farm to a significant business in a single generation and believe the next generation has the energy and passion to take it forward for another generation.'

CHAPTER 6

A.H. BEARD

BEDDING IN THE BLOOD

The E.W Beard & Sons factory replaced the Australian Bedding Mill after it was destroyed by fire in the early 1890s. The photo on the previous page was taken in the late 1890s. The boy on the right is Albert Henry Beard.

THE STORY OF A.H. BEARD began in the late 1880s when Enoch William Beard, a candlemaker, arrived in Sydney after a long journey from Manchester to Australia with his pregnant wife Martha and four children. Martha soon gave birth to a daughter and as the years passed another five children followed, one of whom was Albert Henry Beard.

Shortly after his arrival, Enoch was employed by a real estate agent and a furniture retailer to meet the ships arriving from England and direct new arrivals to their premises. He soon noticed that the new arrivals brought clothes, crockery, ornaments and the odd piece of furniture but no bedding. Recognising an opportunity, he raised finance and established the Australian Bedding Mill to manufacture and sell mattresses.

Disaster struck in the early 1890s when the Australian Bedding Mill was burnt to the ground. Despite not being insured, Enoch was able to rebuild the business as E.W. Beard & Sons, bedding manufacturer and upholsterer.

When Enoch died suddenly in 1899 at the age of only 46, his bedding business was left in the hands of his older sons. His youngest son Albert was only eight years old when his father passed away. Albert began working in the mill in his teens, overseen by his eldest brother Bill who was 17 years his senior. However, it was young Albert who was to follow in his father's footsteps, handcrafting mattresses of the highest quality. Today, Albert's grandsons Garry and Allyn Beard oversee a mattress manufacturing business that employs more than 400 people and makes about 10,000 quality mattresses a week in factories in Sydney, Melbourne, Brisbane, Perth, Adelaide and Hobart, with another in New Zealand.

A new beginning

Disaster struck again in 1926 when the E. W. Beard & Sons factory was destroyed by fire. Albert was forced to rethink his future as the factory was not insured and he was without a job.

During a casual discussion about the consequences of the fire, one of his customers challenged Albert to make six mattresses within a week. He promised that if Albert could meet the challenge, he would pay the full cost on delivery.

With only a gold half sovereign to his name, and without the materials to make the mattresses, Albert was able to convince a supplier to provide him with most of what he needed on credit. With his wife Ada's assistance, Albert met the challenge, paid the debt for the materials and was ready to start his own business. After all, from the time that he started working for his father and older brothers he had been involved in every part of the bedding operation, from making upholstery and mattresses to driving and repairing the company truck.

In 1927, Albert was ready to rebuild his father's business as A.H. Beard. He quickly developed a reputation for making quality handcrafted beds and was able to set up a factory in the garage at the rear of the family home in the Sydney suburb of Sans Souci. By the time the Great Depression began, A.H. Beard had the mattress contract for all the hospitals in Sydney. Albert's grandson, chairman and managing director, Garry Beard, explains:

> 'The hospital mattresses were full of either kapok or horsehair. To save having to purchase new materials, Albert collected the filling, pulled it to pieces and boiled it to meet the hospital specifications for the reuse of bedding materials. He then recovered the material, hand-stitched the mattresses and delivered them back to the hospitals.'

Albert's only son Austin was already working at the factory as a 16-year-old when World War II broke out. Despite his youth, he was already having a significant impact on the family business. Austin was determined to join the armed forces and lied about his age to enlist. He also forged a doctor's certificate to avoid being rejected due to severe acne. When Austin left for Queensland as a signalman his father is reported to have said, 'Don't worry about the business. I'll look after it for you so that when you come back it will still be going.' Austin worked on the telegraph line from Brisbane to Cape York before being deployed in New Guinea.

Kapok

Kapok is a fine, fibrous hair-like substance that grows around the seeds of the ceiba tree, which is found in tropical regions throughout the world including South East Asia, Central America and northern Australia. It is used as a filling for soft toys, cushions and mattresses. Garry Beard explains how it is used. 'You pull it to pieces and then put it into a machine, which beats it repeatedly until it ends up like a cotton wool ball. It was then blown into the mattress cover, which in Albert's time was made like a sausage cover. Ada made the covers on a Singer pedal machine and then Albert would hand-stitch it.'

When Austin returned from service in 1946, he embraced new technology and began to import the latest bedding machinery to make inner spring mattresses. Prior to that the only fillings used were kapok, horsehair and flock. Flock is sheep's wool that is unsuitable for use in the garment industry. Austin's mother Ada was not impressed with his investment as it affected the dividend to the family shareholders. According to Austin's son, Allyn Beard, his father had 'a challenged relationship' with Ada. She was furious when he enlisted in the army and kept a very tight rein on all expenditure, while Austin was very much the entrepreneur and wanted to invest to move the business forward.

Albert enjoyed working on the factory floor with the men and having a beer with them after work. However, his wife Ada thought that he should be more distant from his employees, working in the office and insisting on being addressed as 'Mr Beard'. She is reported to have ruled the expenses with an iron fist and kept a close eye on the bank account and petty cash. Len Cole, the Sydney factory manager for many years, recalls, 'Ada used to total up the handwritten invoices without using a calculator and never ever made a mistake, even in her 70s.' 'Both Albert and my father Austin really struggled with her and dad hated having her questioning and controlling his finances,' says grandson Allyn. 'Despite the strained relationships, the business would not have been here today without Ada,' he reflects.

> The business would not have been here today without Ada.

The market changes

By the early 1950s, there were 14 bedding manufacturers listed in the Sydney "pink pages" phone book; A.H. Beard was facing stiff competition. Albert and Austin became aware of the imminent introduction of a new form of accommodation to Australia known as motels – a composite word deriving from "motor" and "hotels". On hearing about a major development of eight motels being erected by a company named Caravilla in various country towns across New South Wales, Austin spent months patiently calling Caravilla while they were being built. His persistence paid off and A.H. Beard got the order for bedding for the entire project of 88 units. Previously, retail stores supplied mattresses to the motel industry and A.H. Beard became the first factory in Australia to supply its product directly to motels. Sadly, Albert did not live to see the first delivery to a motel as he died of a massive coronary occlusion in March 1956 at the age of 66. The business was left in the capable hands of Austin as managing director and his sisters Joyce, Bev and Ruby as fellow directors.

There was a massive surge in the motel industry in the 1960s and Caravilla was absorbed by its only major rival, Travelodge, which became the leading motel group in Australia. Austin developed a strong rapport with the motel industry after

A.H. Beard's early entry into the market. When Travelodge built the first high-rise motel in Australia, a seven-storey development in Rushcutters Bay, Sydney, A.H. Beard was chosen to supply the bedding. To this day, A.H. Beard supplies bedding for Travelodge Hotels, which currently owns 17 hotels across Australia with more than 3,000 rooms.

In 1962, the factory in Sans Souci that had been used for manufacturing was partially destroyed in a fire. Although it was a temporary setback, Austin took the opportunity to knock down what was left and replace it with a large purpose-built factory that would allow the business to keep up with the growing demand for quality mattresses. In the same year, Gerry Harvey paid a visit to Austin Beard seeking to buy mattresses to extend the range of merchandise in his electrical goods discount store, Norman Ross, into furniture and bedding. A.H. Beard supplied the first 36 mattresses on display in the store, beginning an ongoing business and personal relationship between Gerry Harvey and the Beard family. Harvey Norman (as Norman Ross became) remains one of A.H. Beard's key accounts.

Mopping up the Sans Souci bedding factory after fire had destroyed it.

Family showdown

Garry Beard joined the family business in 1976 when he accepted factory manager Len Cole's offer of a job. He was then taught how to operate every machine on the factory floor. At a directors meeting in March 1977, Austin's sisters Joyce and Bev and his mother Ada, who had bought all of Ruby's shares, demanded that Garry be sacked immediately. Ada and the two sisters did not want the business to continue into the next generation, preferring to reap the benefits of selling it. After a very long and heated debate, Austin was outvoted 3-1 and was ordered to call Garry into the office and tell him his employment with the company was finished. With no explanation for what had just happened, both Garry and Austin sat on the front doorstep of the factory in tears.

Austin stepped back into the directors meeting and resigned on the spot. Upon walking out, he advised Len to stay and make plans with the company. The next day Len called and advised that the entire factory had heard of the upset and said that every employee without exception would give notice to follow Austin and Garry and leave.

Two days later, Lionel Warat of Riley and Albion Pty Ltd, a long-standing supplier of raw materials, called to ask what happened. He had heard on the grapevine that something was amiss at the factory. He wasn't keen about losing one of his best customers. Lionel was from a very wealthy family and asked if Austin would be willing to take the risk and buy out his mother's and sisters' shares if his father Harry agreed to lend him the money. Austin paid Harry a visit and was told, 'Go home, sit down, have a think about what would be a fair offer for the business and come back to see me.' Garry recalls:

> 'Dad, Mum and I sat around the kitchen table with our accountant Tom Vincent and we worked out what we thought was a fair offer.'

On Good Friday 1977, Austin and Garry went to Lionel's home in Point Piper to meet Harry Warat. After a long discussion, the Warat family agreed to provide finance in return for sole supplier rights on some of the raw materials and a floating charge on the business and Austin's family home, including all personal possessions. Fourteen days later, an ultimatum was put to the sisters and Ada. They were advised that they had 24 hours to accept Austin's buyout offer or buy out his shares for the same amount. Austin had three bank cheques for the purchase in hand, the decision was made, and Austin became sole owner of A.H. Beard, albeit with a heavy financial commitment. Garry was immediately reinstated.

Garry's younger brother Allyn believes that the friction between Austin and his mother was a catalyst to his sisters' demands. He says:

'The buyout took a lot of pressure off Dad's shoulders, not having to deal with his mother on a daily basis.'

However, there was more turmoil to come. About six months after the buyout, one of the company's major competitors became aware of the amount of debt that Austin had taken on. Determined to put their rival out of business, they offered to acquire all of A.H. Beard's floor stock from Waltons department store at well under the marked price. Of course, Austin was not in a position to match his competitor's offer and the Waltons account was lost. The competitor then attempted to buy Beard's stock off the floor at Norman Ross but after the personal intervention of Gerry Harvey one model, the Crestfield, was left on the floor. A.H. Beard had lost 80% of its customers. Austin's response was to take Garry out of the factory so that, with the help of salesman Paul Wylde, he could sell the stock destined for Waltons and Norman Ross to furniture and bedding stores across the whole of New South Wales and Canberra. Garry travelled north while Paul headed south. Garry credits the successful sales trip to a combination of determination and the strength of the Beard brand.

The calm after the storm

After the buyout of his aunts, Garry travelled to America to attend an American bedding convention and returned with the idea of finding a franchise brand that would lift A.H. Beard to another level. Shortly afterwards, Therapedic became the business's first American licence, which provided access to innovative technology, better manufacturing techniques and marketing ideas.

When Len Cole left the company in the early 1980s after 20 years of service, Garry stepped into the role of factory manager. In order to keep up with changing trends in mattress design, the business imported a new quilting machine from Italy. An additional factory was leased at Caringbah, about two kilometres south of Sans Souci, to accommodate the large machine. Increasing demand for quality mattresses necessitated expansion to two further premises; this situation began to complicate the flow of production, so the company made the decision to move the whole operation to a single large factory in the suburb of Riverwood.

Meanwhile, new specialty bedding stores were beginning to open and groups such as Sleeping Giant, Sleep Doctor, Captain Snooze and Forty Winks became the biggest sellers of mattress ensembles.

Over the Labour Day long weekend in October 1987, the machinery from Sans Souci and the leased factories was moved to the factory at Riverwood, enabling production to recommence at the new site on the following day. The move left the Sans Souci building empty and Garry successfully applied to the council to rezone the site as residential to maximise its value. The proceeds of the consequent sale of the site were used to pay off the remaining debt to Lionel and Harry Warat, leaving A.H. Beard clear of major financial debt.

When Austin decided to semi-retire in 1988 so that he and his wife could travel, Garry moved into management. But shortly after the couple returned from their first extended holiday, in the Whitsunday Islands, Austin announced that he was officially retiring to Queensland in three months. Three years later, Garry's younger brother Allyn joined the business as marketing manager and since then the brothers have been in control of the business.

Pat Beard

In the late 1940s, Austin met seamstress Eleanor Amy Gray, more commonly known as Pat. She walked past the Sans Souci factory every day on her way to and from work and caught Austin's eye. He struck up a conversation, asked her out, they fell in love and married in July 1949. It was described as a marriage made in heaven – a seamstress and a mattress maker. Without Pat's support it would have been difficult, if not impossible, for Austin to keep the business afloat through the difficult times. Pat was also an unofficial "keeper of the history" of the Beard family and enjoyed recounting stories of the previous generation. Pat passed away on 2 February 2019.

Garry and Allyn have two sisters. Christine worked at the factory and office in her younger days but later joined in the technology revolution and built her own career out of it. Lexie worked alongside her older sister in the factory and office before marrying Alan Bugden at 18 and working in their pool business, Freedom Pools.

The growth spurt

To keep up with the demand created by the number of Harvey Norman and Forty Winks stores opening in Queensland, A.H. Beard leased its first interstate factory in the Brisbane suburb of Geebung in 1995. The new factory allowed for a full production line of the company's whole range of mattresses, apart from the top-quality lines, which were still manufactured at Riverwood. In the same year, Garry was invited to visit the Silent Night factory in Manchester in the UK and accepted an offer of a licence to manufacture and market the brand in Australia and New Zealand. A.H. Beard was able to sub-license Silent Night to Thomas Peacock & Sons in Western Australia and Suparest Bedding in Victoria.

In 1996, Garry and Allyn initiated a period of national and international growth with the opening of a factory in Auckland to enable quicker supply of mattresses to New Zealand. They began negotiations for the purchase of Suparest Bedding, which held the licence of King Koil mattresses throughout Australia. The purchase, which included factories in Victoria and Tasmania along with distribution to South Australia, was finalised in 1997. There were other Australian companies with King Koil licences but they have all been subsequently purchased by A.H. Beard, which is now the sole licensee in Australia and New Zealand.

By 1999, the business had outgrown the factory at Riverwood. By acquiring the 88-year-old bedding company Domino, the major supplier to the Myer and David Jones department stores, A.H. Beard was able to move manufacturing to Domino's larger facility in Padstow.

Another close call

The Domino acquisition was financed by Westpac. With the banking sector under pressure in 2000, the bank insisted on sending in a third-party accounting firm to evaluate the company's position. Their findings led to them to almost closing the company at that time. Westpac requested that its exposure to debt be reduced, which led to both Garry and Allyn selling their family homes to support the business. The bank was not satisfied and froze the company's accounts, giving it 14 days to come up with a plan to trade out of the predicament. The bank attempted to serve Garry with a summons and close the business down, but when the sheriff arrived to deliver the documents, he was greeted by locked gates, lights off, curtains closed – an apparently deserted factory with no letterbox. Group education and development manager, Gillian Wise, reports, 'Little did the sheriff know that Garry was hiding on the floor of his office determined to avoid being served the summons.'

As the bank was preparing to send in liquidators, Garry and Allyn visited family friend Gerry Harvey and his wife Katie Page and explained the company's position. Harvey Norman had a very successful A.H. Beard range in all of its stores and Gerry didn't want to see his supplier go out of business. Garry recalls:

> 'At a meeting in Harvey Norman's boardroom with
> Chairman Gerry Harvey and CFO John Skippen, Gerry
> made the decision to support A.H. Beard. He had John
> phone Westpac to get a payout figure so they could send a
> bank cheque to settle A.H. Beard's account that afternoon.'

After almost losing the family business, Garry and Allyn Beard realised that they needed to implement major changes to ensure a strong future for the business. Since its establishment there had been no regular financial reporting. The business had no accurate knowledge of which lines were profitable and which were not. Garry and Allyn employed a chief financial officer and chief executive officer, which meant non-family members operating the business for the first time in its history. Freed-up from the day-to-day running of the business, the brothers were able to develop a plan for the long-term growth of A.H. Beard. Garry explains:

> 'We needed to bring intellect and experience into the
> business that was more than what we had. What followed
> was a strong period of innovation and expansion with sound
> financial management.'

The board was restructured to include Garry and Allyn Beard, CEO Paul Longman, CFO Paul Hyam and an independent non-executive director Peter Longhurst. 'We learnt from Family Business Australia that to have a full understanding of what is going on you need both family and key executives on the board, so the wavelength is the same,' says Garry.

During this period of growth and change, both Garry and Allyn were, and still are, involved in professional organisations that support either the bedding industry or family businesses. Garry served on the committee of the New South Wales branch of Family Business Australia for 17 years after joining in 1999, including three years as chairman. He is a current member of Family Business Australia's Council of Wisdom. Allyn is deputy chairman of Australian Made Campaign Limited, a not-for-profit public company that encourages consumers to buy Australian products and promotes Australian products at home and throughout the world. He was a member of the International Sleep Products Association Board of Trustees from 2012 until the end of 2018.

Innovations and joint ventures

Allyn's passion for innovation inspired a number of exciting new additions to A.H. Beard's range of products in 2007:

- FlexGel was introduced to the business after Allyn found the product in Salt Lake City, Utah. It was originally used in hospital mattresses in both the USA and Australia because of its high pressure-relieving properties. A.H. Beard's internal testing found it to be ideal for the domestic market, providing body support and superior air flow through the mattress as well as pressure relief.

- Sleep Number was also brought to Australia from the USA. Sleep Number uses adjustable air technology, which allows the customer to adjust the comfort level on each side of a double, queen or king mattress separately with a remote-control device.

- Developed in A.H. Beard's own factory, iComfort is a mattress made of a high resilience foam core, with foam bars that could be added or removed on each side of the mattress to adjust the firmness and support on each side.

The company acquired Adelaide-based Sleephaven Bedding in 2008, completing its national operations and distribution network.

The following year, A.H. Beard opened a joint venture factory in India, in partnership with its foam supplier. The Indian venture was short-lived because without at least five more factories, it could not be profitable. It would have required a large injection of capital and taken a long time to achieve a return. This was a risk that the business was not prepared to take. The company expanded its footprint to the USA in 2010 after signing a licensing agreement with family-owned company Paramount Sleep to manufacture the A.H. Beard brand in its factory in Norfolk, Virginia.

One of the most significant events in the history of A.H. Beard occurred in China when former Prime Minister John Howard officially opened its first store in Shanghai in July 2013. The store was the first of more than 50 A.H. Beard branded bedding stores in China as a joint venture with retailer Shanghai Green Foreign Trade Ltd.

A fresh identity

The acquisition, licensing and creation of new brands – which had grown to 26 in 2008 – along with exports to China and Hong Kong, precipitated the most recent change of location. In 2015, the Sydney factory moved to a larger site, literally across the road from the former Domino factory in Bryant Street, Padstow. By that time the company had recognised the need to consolidate the brands to guarantee the future of the business. The 26 brands were reduced to just six sub-brands under a reinvigorated A.H. Beard master brand.

In 2014, the business launched its fresh identity with an emphasis on educating consumers about the benefits of healthy sleep. Its commitment to sleep education had already become apparent earlier with the launch of the biennial Six Week Sleep Challenge in July 2013. This online program is designed to help participants develop better sleeping habits through weekly challenges. The participants log their progress in an online diary with the aim of successfully meeting each challenge. The program provides an online forum to allow participants to support each other and a blog with expert advice.

Anyone can sign up for the Six Week Sleep Challenge. There is no requirement to own or purchase a bed from A.H. Beard. One incentive to complete the program is a prize of a bed. Garry says:

> 'We conducted a survey of people who have completed the challenge and found that about 30% of them are aware of our brand. But it's not about selling beds. It's about our purpose, improving lives through better sleep.'

As the company's new identity was entrenching itself, unprecedented advances in information technology and smartphones were being made and A.H. Beard was at the forefront of applying cutting edge technology to make "smarter" beds. In 2016, the company introduced its SleepSense bed, which uses a smartphone app to monitor the user's sleep characteristics, including total hours slept, snoring, resting heartrate and sleep efficiency. The information collected can be used to make adjustments to the firmness of each side of the mattress and help improve sleep position and lifestyle habits for better sleep.

In the following year, A.H. Beard developed sleep tracking technology that monitors the bedroom environment and sleeping patterns to provide a detailed nightly analysis. The data recorded, as well as personalised sleep tips and advice, are available through A.H. Beard's Sleep CENTRAL app. As the company website suggests, 'It's like having your very own personal sleep coach in the palm of your hand.' The new products, the A.H. Beard Nox Smart Sleep Light, RestOn Sleep Tracker and Sleep Dot, monitor and record data such as heart rate, respiratory rate, body movements, sleep patterns, light and sound.

Sleep tracker apps 'like your very own personal sleep coach in the palm of your hand'.

New products are being developed and existing products are continually upgraded to take advantage of monitoring technology. The iComfort bed, for example, originally adjusted by adding or removing foam bars now allows the customer to change the firmness of either side of the mattress using a remote control device or smartphone app.

Reflections

Having overcome two "near-death" experiences, there is no doubt that resilience is a major factor in the longevity and success of A.H. Beard. But resilience alone does not explain the remarkable success of this family business in recent years. Even before Albert Beard made his first six mattresses in a week, the family business has had a strong relationship with its suppliers and customers. It is the strength of those relationships that twice saved the company from faltering.

Chairman Garry Beard is keen to acknowledge the often-underestimated contribution of the life partners of all of Enoch Beard's descendants. 'In my case, without the support and love of my wife, Margaret Beard, we would not have achieved the goals we have', he says. He goes on to reflect that passion is essential for the success of any family business. 'We are extremely passionate about what we do,' he says. 'That passion has attracted quality people that have taken this business to another level.' Garry also lists trust, integrity and mutual respect as key ingredients for success.

Group education and development manager, Gillian Wise, who has been working for the business for 25 years, considers herself to be part of the A.H. Beard family. 'Staff see themselves as part of the family because they are treated as family,' says Gillian, and numerous long-serving employees clearly agree.

> This business has something you just can't touch. You can only feel it.

'New employees are welcomed as part of the family and they quickly realise that they are part of it,' says Gillian. The board takes on its own share of the load during difficult times, including working on the factory floor as Albert, Austin, Garry and Allyn have all done. During the Global Financial Crisis they voted themselves a 20% pay cut to avoid retrenching staff.

Neville Middleton has worked for the business for 42 years and has worked in all areas of the factory, including for many years on the quilting machine. He has become known as the company's master of all trades. The man behind the master tape edge machine is Ba, still working for the company after 39 years.

Construction manager, Jonathon Matafa, joined the business as a 15-year-old and is 'the eyes and ears behind our product development' more than 25 years on.

'Every time the Beard story is told, you laugh, you cry and you get a sense of "WOW",' says Gillian, adding, 'This business has something you just can't touch. You can only feel it.' Garry takes great pride in his employees and has a reputation for "tearing up" when he talks about them. Many of them have seen the business through difficult times, including recent flooding when they watched raw materials floating down the street and mud covering the factory floor. Every person is affected when there is an illness or death in the A.H. Beard extended family. Gillian explains the closeness within the business as 'a sense of heart and soul that's been passed on'.

This 1936 Oldsmobile truck, which was used to deliver mattresses, is proudly displayed in the foyer of the A.H. Beard factory at Padstow. Garry (left) and Allyn Beard are shown here taking it on a rare road trip.

Preserving history

After the Great Depression, because of the shortage of coal to generate electricity, the back wheels of the delivery truck were removed in the morning so that a belt could be used to drive a generator for the factory and beds could be manufactured. In the afternoon, the wheels were replaced so that the truck could be used to deliver the beds.

Innovation has been a key element in the success of the business. Garry believes that the "safe to fail" policy established by the board in 2006 has successfully encouraged home-grown innovation at all levels of the business. 'The essence of that policy is in line with Austin Beard's belief that every worker in the factory should be given the opportunity to have a go,' says Garry. One of the best examples of "safe to fail" is the patented Reflex Support Technology, designed and created in A.H. Beard's factory in Padstow and used in the company's popular King Koil range. Reflex responds to the user's size and shape to provide the necessary support. This product has undergone rigorous testing to ensure that it meets the high standards set by the International Chiropractors Association for spinal support, comfort and pressure relief.

A.H. Beard's home-grown "just in time" production model, introduced in 2008, is an innovation that has attracted attention throughout the world. Each mattress destined for Australia or New Zealand is manufactured on demand. When an order is placed with a retailer, it is instantaneously sent to the factory and the manufacturing process begins. The completed product arrives at the store of purchase within three days.

Of course, not every innovation is successful. A venture into waterbeds in the 1980s failed when every one of a thousand heaters and thermostat controls ordered in bulk from the USA proved to be faulty. Six months after the first waterbed was delivered the complaints began to pour in. The serious safety risk to customers left the company no choice but to cease production. Eight years later, A.H. Beard sued the American manufacturer and the matter was settled out of court but after legal fees the amount received was little compensation. Sleep Number adjustable air technology was discontinued when the decline in the Australian dollar in 2014 made it increasingly difficult for A.H. Beard to maintain competitive retail price points and acceptable profit margins.

Garry contends that the most outstanding achievement of A.H. Beard is to have remained in the family for five generations despite all the trials and tribulations. He reflects on one of the highlights:

> 'In 1982, we were chosen to replace the old hard horsehair mattress in the Governor-General's residence in Canberra with a special inner spring mattress to be slept on by Her Majesty, Queen Elizabeth. The staff involved were very proud of their participation in the manufacture of the new mattress, which I delivered personally with a card and a large koala.'

The company has won many awards for design, exports and marketing, including the inaugural Australian Family Business of the Year, presented by Family Business Australia in 1999, and more recently the Mumbrella Award for Insight, an acknowledgement of the value of the Six Week Sleep Challenge and an endorsement of the company's emphasis on sleep education. Garry says that many of those who complete the Six Week Sleep Challenge report improved memory, higher energy levels, better weight management and lower stress levels.

Garry and Allyn Beard agree that being family-owned provides a marketing advantage. 'Consumers like the family story and genuineness of the product. They associate having the family name on the label with integrity,' says Allyn. He adds, 'The Australian Made logo is also very important to our company as we know that it adds credibility to our products and that consumers are influenced positively to purchase a locally made product.'

Moving forward

Despite employing over 450 people in seven sites across Australia and New Zealand, A.H. Beard has maintained its traditional values and continues to honour the legacy of quality and craftsmanship established by its founders. The ongoing success of the business will depend on the ability of the next generation to bring fresh ideas into the business that will keep the company at the forefront of changes in technology and the economy.

Today, while fourth-generation brothers, Garry and Allyn Beard, lead their team, which is challenged to create the best sleep experience available, several members of the fifth generation are already bringing fresh ideas and enthusiasm to the business. Group education and development manager, Gillian Wise, believes the future will be in good hands. She says:

'In 20 years the business may not look like it does now. The fifth generation has vision and will move the business forward. The current leaders will be retired by then.'

Nevertheless, there is a succession plan in place to ensure the future of A.H. Beard remains in the hands of the family and it is reviewed and updated if necessary, every five years. Garry explains how the plan evolved. 'We learnt a lot from Family Business Australia, who helped us develop the succession plan and a family council.' The plan took effect in September 2017. The council consists of adult direct family members only and meets quarterly; it provides a channel of communication between the family and the board. There is also a family forum, which includes partners of family members. The family forum meets with the council annually during the conference of Family Business Australia.

All members of the fifth generation fully understand that they have no obligation to join the business. They also know that if they do, they will only advance through it on merit. However, the passion to maintain their family history and the determination to continue the Australian, family owned business long into the future is very strong in all of them.

Garry's eldest daughter Sally worked as the national training coordinator and has stepped back from the business to start a family. His son Matthew joined the business on a cadetship and has worked his way up to the position of operations manager for New South Wales, the company's largest plant. Anthony, his other son, is following his passion for music and his career as a musician. His youngest daughter Rachel is currently working in the business as the education and development coordinator. Allyn's son Connor works at the factory during holidays while completing a degree in economics.

Lexie and Alan Bugden's younger daughter Hayley pursued a corporate career in marketing where she remained for two decades to become the head of marketing for a global company and is now a member of the A.H. Beard board. Their younger son Adam has followed in his parents' footsteps and was presented with the Australian Pool of the Year Award in 2018 by the Swimming Pool & Spa Association of Australia (SPASA).

The range of products manufactured by the company has been changing for more than 100 years and that will continue with advances in bedding technology and the outcomes of sleep research and development. Gillian predicts:

> 'The type of mattresses we make will change. The technology that already allows consumers to select the right mattress and adjust it to improve their sleep already exists, but it will be continually updated and become more advanced.'

Garry and Allyn Beard are confident that the business will continue to grow and prosper. They agree that the passion that has been behind the business from the very beginning is already evident in the next generation. The A.H. Beard brand is well entrenched throughout Australia and New Zealand and has a presence in China and the USA. The leadership team is making new connections to expand in China and the USA and wants to take the brand to the United Kingdom, Russia, South Korea and other parts of Asia. Indeed, the future looks bright for this family business.

CHAPTER 7

BULLA
DAIRY FOODS

THE CREAM ALWAYS
RISES TO THE TOP

Photo on the previous page shows delivery trucks in the loading bays of the North Melbourne plant in the late 1960s.

THE STORY OF BULLA DAIRY FOODS began in the backyard of a modest house in the Melbourne suburb of Moonee Ponds. Here, in 1910, Thomas Sloan used a wood-fired copper to pasteurise cream in open cans, pioneering a new method of thickening cream. He delivered his cream to his customers in the CBD by horse and cart, with wet hessian bags draped over the cream cans to keep them cool.

Today Bulla Dairy Foods makes more than 250 products, exports to 17 countries and provides employment for approximately 700 workers – a far cry from the one-man operation in a suburban backyard. Thomas Sloan's Bulla Thickened Cream is still the most recognised product of the company he founded.

The early days

Thomas Sloan was aged in his 30s and married with a young family when he created his now famous thickened cream. His father managed several butter factories in Kyneton and Myrniong, rural towns to the north west of Melbourne. As a young man, Thomas managed one of the butter factories and went on to become a milk trader based in Essendon, back in Melbourne.

In the early 1900s, cream was an expensive luxury item and Thomas had the skills and knowledge to manufacture it and build up a profitable business. His brother William supplied Thomas with milk from his dairy near the small town of Bulla, about 20 kilometres north of Moonee Ponds.

In 1912, Thomas went into partnership with North Melbourne businessman, Horace Hillman. The partnership was dissolved after only a few months, with Hillman receiving a generous settlement on the condition that he promised not to set up a cream distribution business within 25 miles of Melbourne's GPO for five years. Shortly afterwards, Thomas registered his manufacturing and distribution business as Bulla Cream Company.

Thomas needed to find a committed partner who would be able to inject capital into the business to make it profitable and sustainable. His brother William declined his offer. He turned to his sister's husband, Hugh Anderson, who had farming experience and agreed to commit himself to the business on a full-time basis. Thomas Sloan and Hugh Anderson became equal partners in the Bulla Cream Company in 1914.

Hugh's capital contribution to the partnership was a former butter factory in Drysdale, near Geelong on Victoria's Bellarine Peninsula, along with a cash payment of £800.

By the beginning of World War I, the dairy farms near Bulla could no longer supply adequate milk to the creamery and it was relocated to the old butter factory at Drysdale. The factory was surrounded by productive dairy farms and its output of cream and butter could be freighted by rail to Melbourne for packaging and distribution.

The first two years of the war coincided with a severe drought in Victoria and many dairy farmers were forced to sell, reducing the supply of milk. However, the Bulla Cream Company was able to survive due to the quality of its cream and ability to help supply butter to England, which was unable to meet its own needs during the war.

A real family affair

In 1918, Hugh Anderson's brother Jack became the third partner in the business after his dairy farm near Koo Wee Rup, 63 kilometres south east of Melbourne, was ruined by the destruction of his entire herd when it was struck with pleuropneumonia. Government compensation for the loss of his herd allowed him to buy into the business. The three partners worked well together. Hugh took charge of the production of cream and butter in Drysdale while his brother Jack and Thomas Sloan marketed and distributed the products from their offices in Melbourne.

The production of cream and butter at the Drysdale factory after World War I was a real family affair. Hugh, his wife and three children lived in a house adjoining the factory and they all participated actively in the business. Hugh's three daughters were often seen churning the butter. His eldest daughter, Anne, was even required to stand in for an often-absent boiler attendant, despite not having the required licence. The involvement of Hugh's family in the long history of the Bulla Dairy Foods business has been nothing short of amazing. Most of his children, grandchildren, great grandchildren, great great grandchildren and even one great great great granddaughter have worked for the company and, today, four generations are still there.

The Bulla Cream Company achieved remarkable change and growth in the 1920s, beginning with the relocation of packaging and distribution to Carlton in 1920 to accommodate increasing demand for cream. The transportation of cream and butter from Drysdale to Carlton in inner city Melbourne was fraught with difficulties, especially in the searing heat of summer. Only eight years later, the Carlton packaging and distribution depot was unable to cope with the volume of production and was relocated to a larger site in Arden Street, North Melbourne, where it remained until 2002.

In 1921, after seven years at Drysdale, the creamery was moved to a dairy farm near Colac in Victoria's Western District, and a year later to East Colac, where a new factory was erected and managed by William Anderson, the brother of Hugh and Jack. Whole milk was delivered to the factory by the Colac Dairying Company. Cream and butter were packed in layers of crushed ice and transported from the factory to Spencer Street railway station in Melbourne, from where it was taken by horse and cart to the Carlton depot.

In 1929, William Anderson formed a partnership with Maurice (Pop) Galway to produce Regal Ice Cream on the site of Colac Ice Works. Maurice had established Colac Ice Works in 1927 to supply the local residences and small businesses with ice for ice chests. The production of ice cream was only a sideline for William and Pop as it could only be done during the warmer months (November to February) and only in Victoria's Western District. The ice cream was sold to shopkeepers in steel cans and could be kept frozen for 24 hours by casing the cans in layers of ice and salt inside wooden barrels.

Delivery cart loaded with cream and butter in Thomas Sloan's Moonee Ponds backyard, circa 1910.

Riding the storms

During the Great Depression of the 1930s the demand for cream, butter and ice cream declined. Although its profits suffered, the Bulla Cream Company weathered the storm better than most. In January 1935, the Bulla Cream Company became incorporated and several months later took over Colac Ice Works from William Anderson and Pop Galway, giving it control of Regal Ice Cream. The acquisition proved to be timely because during hard times people found that ice cream and cream were more affordable as a treat than alternatives like eating out or family trips. It was an inexpensive way to bring some cheer to a difficult period.

Three years later, the East Colac factory was closed and the company relocated to the site of the ice works. It was much more efficient to have the ice and factory on the same site. In 1942, the shareholders of the Bulla Cream Company, all members of the Sloan and Anderson families, transferred the entire business to their newly formed partnership called Regal Cream Products. Despite the restructure, while the Colac-based ice-cream factory was known as Regal Cream Products, the Melbourne-based depots unofficially retained the name Bulla Cream Company.

The outbreak of World War II left the company short-staffed as many of its mostly male employees, including family members, enlisted for war service and served with distinctions. Among them were joint managing director William (Bill) Downey Senior (grandson of Hugh Anderson), who was stationed in Darwin with the RAAF, and Jack Phillips, a future director (son-in-law of Jack Anderson), who was awarded a Distinguished Flying Cross.

Those remaining had to work longer hours under great pressure or relocate to fill gaps left in critical areas. By 1943, the government restricted the domestic consumption of butter, cream and ice cream. Rival company Peters Ice Cream was exempt from rationing so that it could supply Australian and American troops, which left other manufacturers with limited raw materials. Although overall profits at Bulla declined during the last two years of the war, the company was still able to acquire Fergus' Model Dairy in the Melbourne bayside suburb of North Brighton in late 1944. This was done because its bottling facility served as an interim measure until the North Melbourne packaging and distribution site was able to do bottling. The Fergus business was sold to Southern Dairies in 1951 and its bottling manager relocated to Bulla's North Melbourne site.

Founder and chairman of the Bulla Cream Company, Thomas Sloan, died in 1941 at the age of 63 after unsuccessful surgery a year earlier. He left properties in Bulla and Essendon, along with a substantial sum of cash, to his family. Tragically, his youngest son Percival was killed in a plane crash two days after the death of his father while serving with the RAAF in England. Thomas' death was felt deeply within the business that he had founded in 1910 and the communities of Bulla, Essendon and Colac. Thomas had been active in sports clubs and in local government. He was elected to the Council of the Shire of Bulla (now part of Hume City Council) in 1937 and served for two years as Shire President. His obituary in *The Argus* of 29 March 1941 reported:

> 'Mr Sloan started his life with little more than the will to succeed, and by his energies, business acumen and sheer ability and strict integrity, built up the business of the Bulla Cream Company, of which he was the chairman of directors, into a very sound and successful concern.'

Two years later Thomas Sloan's brother-in-law Hugh Anderson passed away, leaving Regal Cream Products in the hands of the next two generations, including Thomas' son Jack Sloan (who had been managing director since 1926), Bill Downey Senior, Keith Anderson and Allan Phillips (Jack Anderson's son-in-law).

Australia's population, relieved after more than a decade of the hardships of the Great Depression and World War II, were ready for a new era with simple pleasures like ice cream on a hot summer's day or whipped cream on a dessert treat. Regal Cream Products was ready to ramp up its production of cream, ice cream and butter. However, the rationing of cream for butter production remained as the Australian government had committed itself to supplying Britain with butter for as long as it was required. In 1946, Regal Cream Products unsuccessfully challenged this commitment in the High Court. However, rather than meekly accepting defeat, the company retained its market lead in cream by manufacturing imitation or "mock" cream, made from vegetable fat rather than butterfat. Its imitation cream, sold under the Bulla brand, remains popular today. It took a change of government in 1948 to finally remove the rationing of cream.

The fabulous 50s and 60s

During the 1950s, the Colac and North Melbourne plants of Regal Cream Products seemed to operate as two separate businesses. Production of cream, ice cream and butter remained in Colac under the management of William Anderson until his death in 1956, after which Bill Downey Senior took over his role of production and operations manager. The North Melbourne depot was the domain of the bottling and distribution to the Melbourne metropolitan area, overseen by managing director Jack Sloan. Regal Ice Cream was exclusively distributed by truck to retail outlets within Victoria's Western District. Despite the operations being some distance apart, they were interdependent and extensive communication between them was vital and mostly achieved by phone.

North Melbourne bottling facility, circa 1960.

Growing up with the business

Bill Downey Senior, a hands-on manager, would often drop into the Colac factory on Saturday mornings to help unload cans of bulk cream or catch up on paperwork, with his young children in tow. His daughter Libby recalls, 'Bill Junior and I ran riot around the factory, playing with the intercoms. Sometimes we went to the freezers and tried not to freeze to the floor in rubber thongs getting an icy pole.' Jack Sloan's son Russell also has fond memories of the 1950s, visiting the North Melbourne depot on Saturday mornings with his father, watching the heavy cans of cream being rolled off the trucks and, like his cousins in Colac, 'playing havoc with the intercom system and getting up to mischief.' Libby, Bill Junior and Russell all joined the business later as young adults.

During the 1950s, the Bulla Cream Company supplied cream to dairies, who sold it to customers, some without refrigerators and still relying on ice chests. The late 1950s and 1960s saw the phenomenal rise of self-service grocers and supermarkets. Bulla was one of the first suppliers to introduce creams into supermarkets and sales rocketed. For the first time, Bulla also sold ice cream outside Victoria's Western District with the introduction of one-quart packages of ice cream called 'bricks', which were sold to self-service grocers and supermarkets. Until the 1960s, ice cream was a seasonal product and throughout the winter months the employees involved were deployed in plant maintenance, painting, concreting, cleaning and other jobs that would keep them busy. Ice-cream workers were never laid off.

In 1960, Bulla moved into markets beyond Victoria, beginning with Sydney, where it opened a storage facility from which it distributed cream to supermarkets. Several years later, the company entered the Adelaide market. By the end of the decade, a purpose-built depot was operating in the Sydney suburb of Ermington and an additional storage and distribution centre had opened in Warrnambool to facilitate sales in Victoria's Western District.

*Delivery of cream from Colac to North Melbourne was subcontracted to
Amezdroz and Menzies of Colac from 1925. These trucks are shown outside the
subcontractor's depot in the early 1960s.*

Consumer demand for ice-cream products increased rapidly
during the 1960s, as the availability of domestic refrigerators
with freezer compartments allowed consumers to store their
frozen treats for long periods. Ice cream could be enjoyed at
home at any time of the year. It was no longer a seasonal product
that could only be enjoyed on summer outings.

The increasing demand necessitated the expansion of the
Colac factory. Bill Downey Senior's brother Jim, a self-taught
refrigeration expert with an inventive mind, was instrumental in
expanding both the factory and the range of ice-cream products.
He designed and built an assortment of machinery to enable the
efficient production of the increasingly popular ice-cream lines
being sold in supermarkets, including a wind tunnel to freeze ice
creams in cones and a chocolate-coating machine.

Full speed ahead

At the end of two decades of increasing profits and considerable change, the company approached the 1970s with a sense of confidence and optimism. However, tragedy struck when Jack Sloan unexpectedly died of a heart attack in July 1970 at the age of only 63. His father had died at the same age. The shock of his loss was deeply felt within the business, especially at the North Melbourne depot, which he had managed for 29 years. Jack had an outgoing personality, a good sense of humour, unwavering commitment and a reputation for being firm but fair. He was well respected inside and outside the company.

Keith Anderson, who had been working at North Melbourne under Jack's direction for many years, and Bill Downey Senior at the Colac factory were appointed as joint managing directors. Despite the distance between them, Keith and Bill Senior communicated extensively, spending hours at a time on the phone.

Jack Anderson's grandson John was instrumental in several innovations in the packaging and marketing of cream and ice cream. The most significant of these was the introduction of non-returnable 10-ounce (approximately 283 gram) plastic bottles for thickened cream in 1971. The new bottles enabled distribution of Bulla cream to cities as far away as Brisbane and Perth, which had previously been impossible because of the cost of freighting it in refrigerated trucks in the heavier glass bottles. Another advantage was the elimination of breakages. John also introduced disposable glass bottles for smaller stores. In 1976, supply of cream from Colac in cans was discontinued and the product was delivered for bottling at North Melbourne in bulk by tankers.

As national sales director, John also introduced the bulk packaging of Bulla's popular stick ice cream and ice confection for supermarkets while its competitors were still only selling those products in milk bars and other small stores. By the mid-1970s, Bulla and Regal ice cream was available to retail outlets and restaurants in bulk cans, tray packs with cardboard lids and as ice-cream cakes. It was popular in sticks and chocolate ice-cream bars, alongside icy poles. Despite this huge range of ice cream and confection, cream was still by far the greatest product by volume coming out the Colac factory.

Bulla took a leap of faith when it followed the advice of John, who proposed – inspired by overseas trends – the introduction of cultured dairy products such as yoghurt and cottage cheese. Joint managing directors, Bill Downey Senior and Keith Anderson, (John's uncle) were reluctant to risk the unknown, but with John's track record of successful innovation they agreed to build a cultured product room at the Colac factory to manufacture yoghurt.

Within two years Bulla won first prize at the Royal Melbourne Show for its reduced fat yogurt, the first of many accolades it has collected for its cultured dairy products. The introduction of cultured products coincided with the Australian public's increasing awareness of the impact of dairy foods on their health. The decision to back John Anderson's proposal was vindicated and, during the 1980s, Bulla manufactured a range of cultured products that included sour cream, cottage cheese and drinking yoghurt as well as the award-winning reduced fat yogurt.

The Colac plant had to be reconfigured to accommodate the manufacture of cultured products, which had to be separated from the production of ice cream and confection because of different temperature and humidity requirements. It was divided into three purpose-designed and separate factories: one for ice-cream production, another for ice confection like stick icy poles and a third for the manufacture of yoghurt and other cultured products.

During the 1990s, Bulla experimented with exporting, first to Singapore and then Japan. In order to satisfy the stringent quality control, health and safety regulations for export to Japan, the procedures at the Colac factory were reassessed and significant changes were made. Workers were required to walk through footbaths before entering certain rooms and wash their hands frequently. The wearing of disposable hair nets, white coats, special shoes, ear muffs and safety glasses became mandatory.

The general manager of operations, Bill Downey Junior, insisted on applying the same standards for all local products and exports to other countries, which by then included China, Indonesia, Malaysia and New Zealand. He is reported to have said, 'If it's good enough for the Japanese why isn't it good enough for our own product?'

Giant steps

In response to the unprecedented growth in product range, volume, staff, customer demand and legal requirements of the 1990s, the company was compelled to undertake a massive restructure. The North Melbourne and Colac sites were unable to keep up with Bulla's growing needs. The North Melbourne site was too small, with a lack of storage and office space. The surrounding laneways couldn't accommodate the bulk cream tankers. They had to unload in busy Arden Street, disrupting local traffic. The Colac site was unable to cope with the increasing demand for ice cream and icy poles, with the added complication of also having to manufacture cultured products like yoghurt and cottage cheese, which required very different production methods and conditions.

In addition, the management structure was outdated, unable to deal with the rapidly changing business, and clearly needed overhauling. The then managing director Russell Sloan explained to staff at the time, 'We're marching up and down on the spot at present. We either go forward or stay the way we are.'

The planning of a new and revitalised Bulla Dairy Foods began in 1996. The first step in what Russell Sloan described as an 'earth shattering' restructure was the introduction of a middle management strand, which included non-family members. For the first time in the history of the company, family members would no longer control all facets of the business. This would allow the directors to focus on strategy and the long-term development of the company. Four committees were set up, each chaired by a member of the board: the Family Business Committee, the Finance, Risk & Environment Committee, the Strategic Marketing & Sales Committee and the Supply Chain Committee.

The second step involved the relocation of all operations except for ice-cream and icy-pole production at the existing Regal Cream factory in Connor Street, Colac. New sites were purchased at Derrimut, a western suburb of Melbourne, and Forest Street, on the outskirts of Colac. A new national distribution centre was constructed at Derrimut at a cost of $8 million. After it opened in October 2001, all goods were transported from Colac to Derrimut, where they were unloaded, stored and then distributed locally, interstate and overseas.

The North Melbourne depot was sold to developers, who later constructed modern apartments on the site. The old Bulla Cream facade was left intact. The Derrimut building was recognised by the Master Builders Association of Victoria with the 2001 award for 'Excellence in Construction of Industrial Buildings Over $5M'.

Derrimut national distribution centre, shortly after it opened in October 2001.

A state-of-the-art factory for the manufacture of cream, imitation cream, sour cream, cottage cheese and yoghurt products was constructed at the Forest Street site at a cost of $30 million. The new plant opened in July 2002, allowing the Connor Street factory to increase its ice-cream and icy-pole production and storage. The North Melbourne cream bottling plant was relocated to Forest Street, where the bottling plant was placed adjacent to the cream processing factory. This eliminated the need for transport of cream in tankers to Melbourne, a distance of more than 150 kilometres, significantly reducing costs.

The decision to make this investment in the regional city of Colac was explained by fifth-generation director, James Downey:

'In theory we could have gone anywhere... but the benefits we receive from the people of Colac outweigh setting up in Melbourne. The country atmosphere and country people are fantastic people to work with. It also ensured the continuation of high-quality production as it not only had ready access to both milk and cream but was surrounded by a workforce that knew the products, the manufacturing processes and the company's work ethic and culture.'

Despite the almost fully automated and computerised manufacturing systems in the new factory, Bulla made a commitment to maintain existing staff levels at Colac. In fact, the number of employees actually increased as the new plant allowed a 50% increase in production. The staff familiarised themselves with computers and more sophisticated control systems and quickly taught themselves to diagnose faults, adapt processes and improve systems, safety and efficiency. James Downey commented, 'This was a true testament to the capabilities of our people. They didn't need to be told what to do. They saw the opportunity for improvement and took it upon themselves because of the pride our employees take in their work.'

From the time the Bulla Cream Company moved to Colac in 1921 it had been supplying ice cream to the Western District of Victoria from its Connor Street factory under the Regal brand. But its customer base was quite small and its ice cream was rarely supplied to supermarkets. The brand was virtually unknown outside the Western District. In 2004, the company decided to rebrand the ice cream manufactured at Connor Street under the Regal brand as Bulla.

The investment continues

Since the restructure that was completed in the early years of the new century, Bulla has continued to invest heavily to take the company to new heights. In 2008, the company acquired Universal Ice Cream, including its factory in the Melbourne suburb of Mulgrave, retaining the whole staff. The factory is now mainly used to produce Bulla's nut-free ice cream. In 2009, the rights to manufacture Cadbury ice cream were obtained with the part-purchase of the West Australian business Fonterra. Cadbury ice-cream production was relocated a year later to a newly built factory on the Connor Street site at Colac. In 2014, Bulla Dairy Foods acquired Rowena Foods, one of the largest manufacturers of the iconic Choc Top range of ice creams. The acquisition included Rowena's factory in the Melbourne suburb of South Dandenong and gave Bulla access to Australian cinemas for the first time. The entire Rowena staff was retained.

The new acquisitions, as well as growth in demand for Bulla's existing products, required a major upgrade to the Forest Street Colac plant. The company invested $7 million in a new cream separating plant, which was commissioned in November 2014. The plant separated milk supplied by more than 50 farms in the district into high-fat cream, skim milk and whole milk for use in the production of cream and ice cream.

Forest Street factory after its upgrade in 2013.

The manufacture of ice cream at the old Connor Street factory used 25% of Colac's entire power supply and was limiting the company's profit. In 2013, Bulla Dairy Foods decided to invest $6.5 million in the construction of an onsite gas-fired power plant. The plant provides the factory's entire base load, provides additional employment and reduces the strain on Colac's power requirements. Its design allows waste heat to produce the steam needed for the ice-cream factory. The plant slashes about $1 million from Bulla's expenditure on power each year and reduces its contribution to carbon emissions.

The investment in the Connor Street factory is seen by the company as a major contribution to the sustainability of both the business and the environment, as well as the bottom line. It reduced the factory's footprint by more than 50%. Bulla is committed to environmental sustainability. 'The Finance, Risk & Environment Committee, formed during the restructure of the business during the late 1990s, oversees a dedicated team who drive reductions in waste to landfill and carbon emissions,' says James Downey.

Reflections

Former managing director, Russell Sloan, grandson of founder Thomas Sloan, believes that one of the key factors in the longevity of Bulla is the stability of leadership. Thomas led the business for 31 years from its inception and was chairman at the time of his sudden death. Russell's father Jack led the company from 1926 for a remarkable 44 years as managing director until he also died suddenly. Jack was followed by Bill Downey Senior and Keith Anderson as joint managing directors until Bill's death, when Keith took on the role alone. Russell reflects, 'Keith Anderson was a remarkably stabilising influence. He started working for the business just before World War II and served the company for 66 years before retiring in 2005 and sadly passed away only two years later,' adding, 'He always treated those connected with the business as extended family.' The current chairman, Ian Sloan, has held that role since 1997, continuing the tradition of stable governance.

At the heart of Bulla's longevity and success is an environment of mutual respect where employees and management have a sense of being part of the family and feel valued, whether family members or not. Many remain with the company for decades.

The retirement of Graeme Hose in 2005 marked the end of 78 consecutive years of employment of at least one member of the Hose family at the Colac factory. Graeme worked at the factory for 42 years. His uncle Alan clocked up a remarkable 57 years and did pretty much everything, working his way up to become manager of the Connor Street ice-cream factory. Graeme was also ice-cream manager. Graeme's father, grandfather and great uncle have all been employees.

The extended family

New employees quickly learn that they are treated as family members. Maurie Finney, having been only recently employed as a mechanic at the North Melbourne depot in the 1960s, contracted tetanus after standing on a nail while working on his car at home. When he returned to work with a paralysed left arm, he fully expected to be fired as he was incapable of carrying out his job. To his surprise, he was given a warm welcome back. Maurie is reported to have said, 'They kept me on. I thought if you ever left Bulla, where would you find a company like that? They'd shoot you out so quick it wouldn't make any difference.' A year later he regained the use of his left arm and was able to resume all of his normal duties. Maurie remained with the company for almost 40 years before retiring.

Russell tells the story of Bert Baker, who worked in the cool rooms at North Melbourne. 'Bert lived just around the corner from the depot and used to come in at night to unload the cream cans off the truck as they came in from Colac so they were ready for processing the next day. The driver would slide cans down the ramp and Bert would kick it or shove it into the exact right spot in the cool room.' Bert's wife Annie was the tea lady at the depot for many years. 'She was still cheerfully serving tea and coffee well into her 90s despite being unable to climb the stairs to the upstairs offices,' says Russell.

Until the mid-1960s, the Colac factory was an exclusively male domain. Some women worked in the office at North Melbourne and two ladies were working on the bottling line. One of them was reputedly as good as two men taking bottles off the line and putting them into crates. But it wasn't long before Bulla began to provide opportunities for women to operate machinery and do some of the "heavier" work such as lifting cream cans for pouring into a vat.

By the turn of the century, women held senior positions at the Colac factory and the North Melbourne depot. The first female to be appointed to the board of directors was Denise Fankhauser, daughter of Keith Anderson, in 2005. Denise remains on the board today and is currently chair of the Finance, Risk & Environment Committee.

Russell reflects:

> 'There has been an element of luck in our ability to survive for 110 years. But we've done much more than survive. We've achieved great success and continue to grow.'

He contends that the winning formula for success has involved the loyalty of family members and the constant reinvestment into the business.

According to Russell, the purpose of the company, expressed in a document signed by all six current directors, encapsulates the values exemplified by the families since 1910:

* *We are the enemies of family unfriendly practices, selling the farm and those who short-change Australia's future for their profit today.*

* *We refuse to cut corners, we don't accept the 'good enoughs' or waste in any form.*

* *We take pride in our craftmanship and passion, and pleasure from a job well done.*

* *We act with integrity and generosity of spirit to deliver a sustainable profit with thought for family, community and the world of tomorrow.*

* *Our mission is to ignite passion for real dairy food and celebrate family life today and always.*

Since the turn of the century, the business has been governed by a six-member board comprising two descendants from each of the Sloan, Anderson and Downey families, all descendants of founder Thomas Sloan and his partners, Hugh and Jack Anderson. When Russell Sloan retired as managing director in 2010, the board acknowledged that his best replacement might be found outside the family. Reg Weine, general manager of marketing, sales and innovation, was appointed as CEO. Ian Sloan remained in the role of chairman. When Reg resigned to take up the position of managing director of SPC Ardmona, he was replaced by another non-family member, current CEO Allan Hood.

Russell believes that it is important to keep personal family matters separate from the business. 'It's something that our predecessors did well and we intend to make sure that we follow their example,' he says.

The innovations and new product development that occurred in the 1970s and 1980s were largely in response to changes in consumer demand, the initiatives of marketing manager John Anderson and trust placed in him by his uncle Keith and Bill Downey Senior. Reflecting on that period, Russell says, 'It was a period of rapid expansion and was critical to the growth of the company. It put us at the forefront of Australian dairy production.'

One of the most important innovations was the change from glass to plastic cream bottles in 1971. It was believed to be a world-first. It took the company eight years to develop a container that was hygienic and could be filled and capped by machines. More recent innovations include flavoured creams, lamington flavoured ice cream, fairy bread ice-cream sticks, gluten-free ice cream and nut-free ice cream.

Bulla has won numerous awards for its range of products, particularly for its innovative creams and cottage cheese, but according to Russell the company's biggest achievement is being named by Roy Morgan Research as the most popular brand of ice cream ahead of Peters and Streets, both owned by huge overseas companies. Russell declares:

'Successfully competing with some of the largest companies in the world is a tribute to the dedication of family and employees.'

Bulla remains one of the top three manufacturers of ice cream in Australia and has been the most popular brand of cottage cheese for many years. 'We've been the largest supplier of table cream in the southern hemisphere since 1998,' says Russell.

Moving forward

Bulla Dairy Foods looks to the future with confidence and optimism, just as it did at the dawn of the 1970s. 'The company has little debt, a dedicated and passionate workforce and cohesive leadership. The Colac factories and Melbourne factories and distribution centres are capable of meeting the company's needs for many years to come,' says Russell Sloan. His fellow director, James Downey, adds, 'We have a long history as a business, yet we remain on the cutting edge. We are not afraid of the future.'

Until recently, leadership was passed down through the Sloan, Anderson and Downey families. It worked because there was always a family member with the experience and qualifications to step into key roles when necessary. However, as the business grew and became more complex it was apparent that this ad hoc method of passing the baton could not continue.

> Being a member of the founding families should not provide a free ride.

Russell says, 'Being a member of the founding families should not provide a free ride.' He remembers feeling very unpopular when he told his three sons that if they wanted to work in the business they would first have to get a university degree and then work somewhere else to get relevant experience. From his own experience he knows how working elsewhere has benefitted both himself and the company to this day.

Russell's eldest son David completed a degree in commerce and worked for five years at Fonterra's Bonland Dairies before joining Bulla Dairy Foods as an account manager. Since then he has worked his way up to the role of general manager of sales and has obtained an MBA at the University of Sydney. Youngest son Alistair holds Bachelor of Business (HR) and a Master of Business Systems degrees. Prior to joining Bulla, he worked with HR consulting firm Mercers for several years. At Bulla he has held roles in sales, finance, new product development and strategy, and is currently General Manager, People & Culture. Russell's other son Rob holds a Bachelor of Business (Sports Management) degree and is a Graduate of the Australian Institute of Company Directors. Although he is currently a successful radio executive he has a keen interest in the company and keeps a close eye on its performance.

Members of the pioneering Sloan and Anderson families currently hold positions in the business ranging from factory hand to laboratory assistant to managers and directors. More than half of them are women. The sixth generation of the Anderson family is already represented in the business by Hugh's great great great granddaughter, Daisy Downey, who is a factory hand at Forest Street in Colac.

In 2011, the family constitution formalised a succession plan that encourages family members to become employees and specifies that employment is by merit. Applicants who are family members must be qualified and meet the expectations of the role. It is only if two equal candidates can't be split that a family member is given preference.

Bulla Dairy Foods has been approached many times in recent years with offers to buy the business. But the Sloan, Anderson and Downey families are united in their firm opposition to selling. 'The business is firing on all cylinders and has the potential to reach greater heights, including expanding our export markets,' says Russell. Bulla has managed to survive through changes in technology, manufacturing processes, the marketplace and government regulations as well as two World Wars, a major depression and other economic downturns. The company has responded successfully to every challenge it has faced, including several long periods of drought to which the dairy industry is especially vulnerable. 'We're faster and more nimble than our competitors,' says Russell. 'As a family business we're passionate about what we do and work together as a team.'

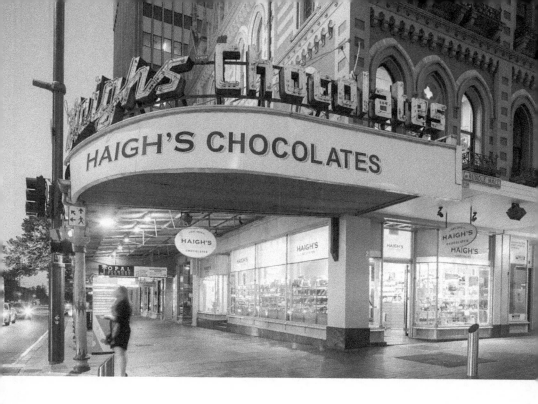

CHAPTER 8

HAIGH'S CHOCOLATES

JOURNEY TO PERFECTION

Photo on the previous page shows the Haigh's Beehive Corner store today.

THE HAIGH FAMILY has been seducing Australian consumers with its delectable confectionery and chocolates since 1915, when Alfred E. Haigh opened his store at 34 King William Street in the iconic Beehive Building in Adelaide's CBD. Today, Haigh's is Australia's oldest family-owned chocolate maker, creating enticing chocolate treats manufactured in Adelaide from premium cocoa beans sourced from plantations around the world.

Haigh's original Beehive Corner store in Adelaide is now one of 18 retail stores in cleverly selected sites, including the heritage-listed Block Arcade in Melbourne and the magnificent Queen Victoria Building in Sydney. Haigh's Visitor Centre is one of the most popular tourist attractions in Adelaide with free factory tours, chocolate tasting and its own retail outlet. There is also an online store on the company's website.

Humble beginnings and grand plans

Alfred E. Haigh was born in Adelaide in 1877 and was educated at Jamestown in South Australia's mid-north where, at the age of 19, he opened his first fruit and confectionery shop. He supplemented locally grown fruit and vegetables with confectionery railed from Adelaide along with his own home-made boiled sweets. After marrying in 1902, Alfred spent several months in Western Australia before returning to his home state, where he worked for a farm machinery company until deciding that the confectionery business was where he belonged.

With his wife Lettie and infant son Claude, Alfred moved to Mount Gambier in 1905, where he opened a fruit and confectionery shop in the town's main street. Alfred's entrepreneurial flair quickly became apparent when he secured the rights to operate fruit and refreshment stalls at local meetings and events, including horse racing and the annual show. He added ice cream and soft drinks to his range of products in about 1909, selling them from a cart in the main street; he established a soft drink factory nearby. By then Alfred and Lettie had an infant daughter Alvina.

Alfred expanded his business by opening new fruit and confectionery stores in 1911 and 1912 in the towns of Pinnaroo and Lameroo, both about 350 kilometres north of Mount Gambier, along with a similar store in Unley Road, Adelaide, in which he and Lettie worked. After closing the Unley Road shop he opened another in Henley Beach Road. Because all of the stores were on the railway network, Alfred was able to make regular train trips to keep a close eye on them.

Britain's declaration of war on Germany in August 1914 paved the way for an opportunity that Alfred E. Haigh could neither have anticipated nor resisted. At a time when Alfred was already expanding his business, German-born Carl Stratmann had opened a chocolate and confectionery shop in Adelaide's Beehive Building (in September 1913) and was making and selling chocolate and confectionery of the highest calibre. Carl was a highly skilled chocolatier and had served a long apprenticeship in Europe before moving to Australia to work for MacRobertson Chocolates.

But, by 1915, anti-German sentiment perpetuated by the press bordered on hysteria. German migrants were looked upon with suspicion and distain. Town and street names with German origins were changed. Germans in Australia who were of a suitable age to join the army were interned in concentration camps. Others were sacked from their jobs or had their businesses ruined. Carl was faced with newspaper advertisements urging the boycott of businesses owned by German migrants and was forced to sell his business. Alfred was fortunate to be in a position to buy it, including the stock, leasehold, professional manuals, recipes, manufacturing equipment and a collection of moulds.

Carl's invaluable assistant, Mabel Leslie, chose to continue working at the shop and remained with the company for many years. Whether Mabel's decision was just a stroke of luck or influenced by Alfred's business acumen is not known, but the continuing growth and success of his enterprise suggests that it was the latter.

In the early years of his Beehive Building shop, Alfred was selling confectionery, including chocolate, produced by an assortment of Australian and overseas manufacturers, along with his own boiled sweets and chocolate creations made in an upstairs room with the help of Lettie. Among Alfred's earliest chocolate products were novelty chocolates in the shape of animals, using Stratmann's moulds.

Alfred was intent on expanding his business, while at the same time making a name for himself as the best confectioner in South Australia. Competition was fierce but very few confectioners specialised in chocolate. Alfred decided that with his rare collection of recipes, manuals and equipment he could realise his goal by manufacturing a range of high-quality chocolate products and selling them in his own shop. He experimented with coating dried pineapple, dried apricots, dried pears and other dried fruits in dark chocolate and put them together in a hand-made box labelled as Haigh's Fruit Chocolate Assortment, which until 2018 was still being sold as Haigh's Original Fruits Assortment.

Theatre boxes

Recognising the emerging popularity of silent film pictures, Alfred introduced theatre boxes, which contained both sweets and chocolates including his new fruit-centred creations. A theatre box was the perfect gift for a sweetheart or an indulgent treat for couples enjoying a night at the theatre or movies.

World War I provided an unexpected boost to Haigh's and other Australian confectionery businesses. Treats such as biscuits, sweets and chocolate provided a convenient and effective way for mothers to send their love to their sons at the front. A number of "comfort funds" were established to raise money or send gifts such as newspapers, cigarettes and confectionery to troops serving overseas.

Alfred's ambition and initiatives were already paying dividends. By 1917, his profits had enabled him to purchase two adjoining properties in the suburb of Parkside, little more than one kilometre from the centre of Adelaide's CBD. Alfred and his family moved into the house on one of the properties. He built a small two-roomed factory on the other and moved all manufacturing operations there from the room above his shop in 1919.

Shortly after the end of World War I, Alfred opened a new fruit and confectionery shop just over a block from his shop in the Beehive Building. It included a refreshment room, which boasted a soda fountain, two aerators, a marble-topped counter and tables to match and an ice-cream cabinet. He sold his Mount Gambier business and brought Harold Lewis to Adelaide as an assistant to his factory manager, W.A.E. Smith. Harold had begun working for Alfred in Mount Gambier as a 14-year-old in 1911.

The roaring twenties

By 1920, Alfred had already made his mark on the South Australian confectionery industry – from the 19-year-old boiled sweet maker and shopkeeper in a small town to owner of a thriving business, a house, a factory, and father of two children.

Throughout the 1920s, Alfred's untiring ambition and astuteness drove his business to further success. In 1920, he acquired new machinery from the USA, England and local sources. His investment in state-of-the-art machinery continued throughout the decade, increasing both the range and quality of his chocolates and other confectionery.

When his only son Claude entered the family business in 1921 as a partner at the age of 17, Alfred was only in his 40s and still had plenty of energy and ideas. He recognised that he could make far superior moulded and chocolate-coated products from raw cocoa beans, instead of using imported block chocolate. Alfred began blending different varieties of imported beans and developed his own roasting and grinding techniques in his Parkside factory in 1921. Fortuitously, at about the same time, an Australian government increase on the duty on imports of confectionery including chocolate had damaged Alfred's competition. In addition, there was no duty levied on imported cocoa beans, which made his new process quite profitable.

In the early 1920s, Alfred began what was to become a remarkably successful secondary career as a property developer and landlord. He purchased a block of land at the beachside suburb of Henley Beach, on which he constructed an impressive building named Haigh Mansions, which housed eight fully-furnished flats for letting. In 1922, he purchased a building at 41 Rundle Street, less than 150 metres from Beehive Corner. Alfred promptly demolished it and constructed a five-storey building with a basement. The building soon became a sought-after business address never short of reliable tenants.

> Café Wattle, in the basement of the [Haigh's] building, was recognised as the best place in Adelaide for lunch, afternoon tea and supper.

By 1927, Alfred had purchased the property behind it and constructed another five-storey building, with walkways connecting the two buildings on each floor. The whole complex became known as the Haigh's Building and became associated with charm, style and elegance. When Alfred later opened Café Wattle in the basement of the building it was recognised as the best place in Adelaide for lunch, afternoon tea and supper. The Haigh's

Building was sold in 1955 and is now known as Garko House. The building was heritage listed in 2001.

The Haigh's Beehive Corner store in the 1920s.

During the 1920s, Alfred leased a property in Adelaide's main shopping strip, Rundle Street, which included a shop at street level. He sub-leased two rooms above the shop. He continued to expand the Parkside factory by buying adjoining properties and added a separate plant to manufacture the elaborate cardboard boxes for Haigh's Chocolates, with lids adorned with various scenes and Art Deco pictures. He later added beautifully coloured prints of flowers to the lids.

Also during the 1920s, Alfred expanded his retail network to rural South Australia by selling chocolates through existing outlets in Kapunda, Gawler and Clare. In 1928, he acquired the sole right to sell confectionery at all cricket and football matches at the Adelaide Oval. With crowds of tens of thousands at local football games and up to 50,000 for cricket test matches, this was a very lucrative deal. What was originally a three-year contract remained in place until the early 1980s. By 1930, Alfred had opened three new shops: at Jetty Road in Glenelg, King William Street in Adelaide and in Broken Hill.

Alfred's interest in horses, developed as a young boy in Jamestown, was rekindled when horse racing became more accessible to the public through radio broadcasts. In 1927, in partnership with W. A. E. Smith, Alfred purchased his first racehorse, King's Colors. What began as a small investment in one thoroughbred grew into a stable of several horses. Two years later, he purchased an 859-acre property at Mallala, about 58 kilometres north of Adelaide, to accommodate his growing racing stable.

The Great Depression hit Adelaide more severely than most of Australia, forcing numerous retrenchments and factory closures. When the resulting poverty and unemployment caused the demand for chocolates and other confectionery to plummet, Alfred's response was to reduce the production of his luxurious and expensive chocolate boxes and increase the production of cheaper items such as his penny chocolate frogs, rather than reduce staff. In addition, he expanded his retail network by supplying cafés and other retailers in the regional South Australian towns of Port Elliot, Port Pirie, Mount Gambier, Loxton and Wallaroo.

An unexpected transition

When Alfred died unexpectedly and suddenly of a heart attack at the age of 56 in 1933, control of the business and stable of six thoroughbred fillies passed on to his only son Claude, in keeping with the tradition of the time. The property at Mallala was left to Lettie.

Although Claude had little interest in making confectionery or chocolate, he had been working in the business for 12 years as a partner and accountant. His only formal training was as a bookkeeper with a shipping agent and he was more cautious and conservative than his father. Claude's real passion was breeding and racing thoroughbreds. In 1934, he established a stud, which he named Balcrest, in the Adelaide Hills, taking the family's interests in horses to a whole new level. Claude served on several racing industry committees and eventually became Chairman of the Adelaide Racing Club, an office he held from 1969 to 1973. Balcrest remains in the family today and Claude's son John, grandsons Alister and Simon, and granddaughter Sara take an active interest in the stud.

Claude and his wife Gerta shared a love of gardening and regularly opened up their extensive gardens of rhododendrons, azaleas, lilacs and daffodils at their Adelaide Hills home to the public to raise money for the local kindergarten and charities. Claude also donated fillies for auction at country racing clubs to raise funds for Legacy.

Despite Claude's preoccupation with breeding and racing horses, he continued to take an active role in Haigh's chocolate businesses. In fact, it was Claude and factory manager Harold Lewis who kept the business afloat during the long and painful recovery from the Great Depression and World War II. With sales diminishing in 1940, Claude leased half of the Beehive Building shop to a handbag and hosiery business. Despite government price control on confectionery and sugar rationing, the production of confectionery, including chocolate, at Haigh's remained relatively constant throughout World War II. Because Haigh's was manufacturing for the troops, it was partially exempt from sugar rationing. In addition, the company made shrewd decisions about which lines should be maintained, increased, decreased or dropped completely for customers at home.

The influx of American servicemen after the Pearl Harbor attack of December 1941 increased the demand for confectionery. Lower ranked American soldiers earned twice as much as their Australian equivalents and were inclined to spend freely on luxury items such as sweets and chocolate. In addition, imports of confectionery diminished significantly midway through the war, leaving Australian consumers reliant on locally manufactured products.

> The influx of American servicemen after the Pearl Harbor attack of December 1941 increased the demand for confectionery.

At the end of World War II, Haigh's stores were quite different from those of today. About half of the stock was chocolate. The remainder consisted of mints, jubes, toffees and other confectionery, some of it imported. The stores also sold milkshakes and spiders (ice-cream sodas in the USA). Cake lines had been discontinued in 1939.

Only two new Haigh's shops opened during the 1930s and 1940s but the registered offices were moved from the Haigh's Building to the Parkside factory. In 1950, the family purchased a freehold interest in the Beehive Building, which housed the original "jewel in the crown" of Haigh's stores.

Claude's only son John Haigh joined the business in early 1946 after his father experienced an apparently heart-related health scare. At the age of only 16, John had just completed his secondary education and had no plans for tertiary education or a career. Claude realised that he would soon have to reduce his active involvement in the confectionery business and set John to work in the factory. As a factory hand he worked his way through every part of the factory and, under the watchful eye of Harold Lewis, learnt how to make every single product in the Haigh's range of chocolates and other confectionery. Like his grandfather Alfred, John had a fascination for chocolate and believed that was where Haigh's future would lie. Although still in his teens, John began to have an impact on production and by 1949, the production of chocolate confectionery exceeded that of non-chocolate confectionery for the first time.

Taking chocolate to new heights

John was ambitious, energetic, shrewd and keen to learn more. He had a vision to take Haigh's to new heights in chocolate making and secured a job in the Lindt factory in Switzerland, beginning in February 1950, where he could learn from the masters. During his ten months at Lindt, John worked in every part of the factory, watching and learning the whole time.

Upon leaving Switzerland, John aimed to take full advantage of the contacts he had made and travelled to London to meet with the agents who supplied Lindt with cocoa beans. He successfully negotiated for Haigh's to import beans of the same quality from South America and Ghana. With a lust for chocolate manufacturing excellence, John also visited the USA to look at production methods, retailing strategies and marketing.

After returning to Adelaide in 1951, John overhauled the chocolate-making process by purchasing new machinery to take advantage of the higher quality beans that he was able to import through Lindt's agent. The office was moved out of the factory to the cottages next door to accommodate the new equipment. At the same time, John reintroduced two of Haigh's most popular lines, chocolate fruits and gift boxes, started advertising in the daily press and redesigned the packaging. During the 1960s, the name Haigh's Chocolates quietly began to appear on some of the company's stationery, reflecting John's focus on chocolate.

The ice cream came from Adelaide dairy company AMSCOL, to whom Haigh's had been supplying chocolate for its popular chocolate-coated ice cream known as Dairy Chocs since the late

1940s. During the 1950s and 1960s, the two companies had a collaborative relationship. AMSCOL was provided with chocolate for its chocolate-coated ice creams and in exchange Haigh's received large vats of cream for its fudge-centred chocolates and ice cream for its own choc-tops.

Haigh's at the movies

In 1954, together with his father Claude, who still occupied the position of managing director, John undertook an ambitious retail expansion program that was to last almost 15 years. It began with the sale of Haigh's confectionery at picture theatres in Adelaide and Mount Gambier and was followed by the opening of three new retail stores in strategic locations. In 1958, Claude and John set up a new partnership, Haigh's Theatre Shops, which sold confectionery – including the obligatory Jaffas and Fantales – along with ice cream in 20 cinemas, all in South Australia, by 1960.

In 1959, Claude handed the role of managing director to John so that he could concentrate on his greatest passion, the racing and breeding of thoroughbreds. Claude had a stroke in 1975 and died in November 1980. As was the custom at that time, the eldest son John inherited some shares, while others were held in family trusts. Surviving daughters Margaret and Rosemary were given shares in other companies that owned an assortment of properties.

One of the immediate challenges faced by the newly appointed managing director was the introduction of television to Adelaide in 1959 and its impact on the popularity of cinemas. Haigh's had become reliant on its picture theatre outlets and sales were declining rapidly as the population became infatuated with the small screen. John Haigh's response was to gradually sell off the less profitable theatre shops and most were gone by 1965, the same year that Haigh's opened its first interstate store at the exclusive "Paris end" of Collins Street in Melbourne. Later that year, the company opened another Melbourne shop in the equally fashionable South Yarra, along with a counter in the prestigious department store Georges. Over the next decade, additional shops were opened in Adelaide and its suburbs. Less profitable shops were closed or strategically relocated.

John was well-equipped to take advantage of both the benefits and new challenges that lay ahead with the rapid social change of the late 20th century. His goal was to make chocolate equal to the very best in the world. John continued to invest in better and more modern equipment to improve the manufacturing process and, ultimately, produce better quality chocolate. Haigh's non-chocolate confectionery was gradually phased out during the 1980s and 1990s and by March 1993 it had completely disappeared from the shops.

In 1987, marketing manager Stuart Chandler made an arrangement to supply chocolate to a Perth boutique, Tivoli Chocolates in Perth's trendy London Court. The choice of location for this venture seemed ideal but the experiment was abandoned after only a few months because of inadequate space to store the required quantities, not to mention the melting of several deliveries of chocolate in 40-degree temperatures outside the store.

Determined to expand the business beyond South Australia and certainly more inclined to take risks than his father Claude, in the following year John accepted an invitation to open a Haigh's store in a shopping centre on the Gold Coast. However, a series of events seemed to conspire against the success of this store, including poor management of the shopping centre, competition from the much larger Pacific Fair shopping centre, a downturn in Japanese tourism and the melting of chocolates left in the sun at the airport before delivery. The Gold Coast store closed in 1992, less than four years after opening.

The internal fittings of the unprofitable Gold Coast store were immediately relocated to set up a new store in the Block Arcade in Melbourne's CBD. This location was keenly sought after by marketing manager Stuart Chandler and was the perfect fit for Haigh's Chocolates. Built in the 1890s and modelled on Milan's grand Galleria Vittorio Emanuele, the Block Arcade is the home of prestigious boutiques and quaint cafés and is still one of Melbourne's favourite places to shop and be seen.

The Haigh's store in Melbourne's heritage listed Block Arcade (2014).

Generation four: The brothers

Having succeeded in transforming Haigh's into a world-class chocolate manufacturer and retailer, John retired as managing director in 1990, handing the reins over to his two sons, Alister and Simon. Alister had joined the business in 1973 at the age of 18 after spending his first year after secondary school in horse-related employment. He worked as a jackaroo on the edge of outback South Australia, next at the Te Parae horse stud in New Zealand and then travelled to England to take possession of a new stallion destined for Balcrest Stud. Simon joined the business in 1977 after also spending a year working at Te Parae.

He embarked on a science degree but a few months studying at the University of Adelaide was enough to discourage him from that pursuit. Simon recalls, 'After earning money and being independent for a year, being a broke student wasn't for me.'

Both Alister and Simon worked their way through all areas of the factory before moving into the office. Alister went on to become company secretary, factory manager and then general manager of Haigh's in 1984. Simon divided his time between chocolate making in the factory, managing the company's books and looking after IT requirements. John continued to take an active role in the business as chairman of Haigh's Chocolates, a position that even now, in his 90s, he still holds. He also retains an active interest in Balcrest and its thoroughbreds.

John's accomplishments as managing director left Alister and Simon with a very hard act to follow. Fortunately, their skills and talents complemented each other. Alister assumed control of general management while Simon became responsible for finance, information technology and technical operations. In 1997, Alister became chief executive officer, while Simon took the role of chief financial officer. Together, they make a great double act.

Alister and Simon streamlined the manufacturing process and created a strong and uniform retail image for Haigh's Chocolates as an Australian company of distinction, class and excellence. In 1990, when Alister and Simon took charge, each store had a different design and colour scheme. All existing stores underwent a major refurbishment with a uniform design that radiated warmth and classic elegance. The same image was projected in all new stores, and in packaging with a new logo.

With healthy growth in sales and the number of products, the Parkside factory was bursting at the seams. A new warehouse in the nearby suburb of Keswick was leased in 1994 and two years later the Parkside factory was extended. A neighbouring property was purchased to house new offices and new stores were rolled out in Adelaide, Melbourne, Sydney and, more recently, Canberra. A new warehouse and additional factory were established in 2003 and a new Distribution Centre opened in 2010, all in the inner Adelaide suburb of Mile End.

Inspired by factory tours overseas and in Australia, Alister and Simon opened a Visitor Centre in December 1995, which allows visitors to see the manufacturing process and includes a retail outlet. The Haigh's Chocolates Visitor Centre quickly became a popular destination for interstate and overseas tourists as well as a favourite outing for locals. The tours were and remain especially popular with international and national conference delegates. The Visitor Centre currently hosts up to seven free guided factory tours each day.

In keeping with its refreshed and now consistent public image portrayed by its refurbished stores and products, Haigh's Chocolates took its marketing and promotional activities to a new level, participating in public events such as art gallery exhibitions and gourmet food events, featuring exclusive Haigh's chocolate delights especially created for each event. This initiative began with the Art Gallery of South Australia's exhibition 'Monet and Impressionism from the Holmes à Court Collection' in 1991, for which Haigh's created special boxes of premium chocolates featuring Monet prints on the lids. Similar special event partnerships with iconic hotels such as the elegant Mount Lofty House in the Adelaide Hills and the heritage-listed Windsor Hotel in Melbourne followed.

Haigh's expansion under the leadership of the brothers has been nothing short of astonishing. At the beginning of 2019, Haigh's Chocolates had about 650 employees spread over three states and Canberra. The majority are in Adelaide, staffing the

> Haigh's expansion under the leadership of the brothers has been nothing short of astonishing.

offices, the factories, the warehouses and Distribution Centre and the stores.

Haigh's is on a mission to deliver a world-class experience to its customers and the vehicles for that mission are its staff and corporate identity. The fuel consists of the very best ingredients, including premium cocoa beans, specialised chocolate making techniques and attention to detail in customer service and packaging.

Haigh's Chocolates is now recognised as the manufacturer of the best chocolate in Australia and its reputation has been reinforced with medals and trophies at the Royal Melbourne, Sydney and Adelaide Shows. The company has also been recognised as an employer, winning the Prime Minister's Employer of the Year Award in the medium business category for South Australia in 2001, 2003 and 2005 and inducted into its Hall of Fame in 2005. In 1993, John Haigh was personally honoured with the Alfred Stauder Award for Excellence in acknowledgment of his significant contribution to the Australian confectionery industry. Simon Haigh is immensely proud that Haigh's Chocolates was listed among the best producers of chocolate manufactured from bean to product at the 2014 World Chocolate Awards. He says:

> 'Being judged alongside the best in the world in an independent competition makes me very proud of what we have achieved.'

Community and environmental responsibility

Over the years, Haigh's Chocolates has been an enthusiastic and generous supporter of a range of charitable and cultural organisations, community projects and environmental initiatives, by providing donations of products, part-proceeds of sales and assistance with fundraising. The present focus is on Variety, which provides programs and events to enrich the lives of children who are sick, disadvantaged or have special needs. Other organisations among the many supported by Haigh's include the Adelaide Symphony Orchestra, the State Theatre Company of South Australia and Zoos South Australia. Simon Haigh explains:

> 'We research what we contribute to and tend to raise funds rather than just donate a sum of money. Putting money back into the community does make you feel good.'

Haigh's commitment to the environment is demonstrated by positive action and staff are encouraged to be involved by offering suggestions to improve work practices to benefit the environment. Among the many initiatives taken so far are:

- installation of underground storage tanks to collect rainwater falling off the factory roof for use in the steam boiler system

- the use of 100% recyclable materials in all packaging

- reusing bubble wrap used to protect products during transportation or donating it to neighbouring businesses for their packaging

- the use of biodegradable cellophane bags, wrapping paper and paper bags.

Haigh's is an original signatory to the Australian Packaging Covenant, an industry and government initiative to reduce the environmental effects of packaging on the environment.

Because Australia does not have a viable cocoa growing industry, all of the beans used in Haigh's chocolate manufacturing process are imported, mostly from South America, Africa and the Pacific. The company has committed itself to support sustainable farming practices and most of the beans it sources are from farms that are UTZ certified, a program now part of the Rainforest Alliance.

Haigh's is also a participant in global partnerships with governments, non-government organisations and industry, including the International Cocoa Initiative to improve the lives of West African cocoa farmers and their families through a public certification process. It is a member of the World Cocoa Foundation which works in all cocoa growing regions to help farming communities.

Supporting Australian fauna

In 1993, Haigh's Chocolates created a chocolate Easter Bilby and joined forces with the Foundation for Rabbit Free Australia (RFA) to raise awareness of the damage done by rabbits to native wildlife and help 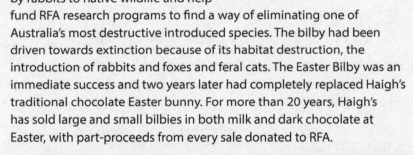 fund RFA research programs to find a way of eliminating one of Australia's most destructive introduced species. The bilby had been driven towards extinction because of its habitat destruction, the introduction of rabbits and foxes and feral cats. The Easter Bilby was an immediate success and two years later had completely replaced Haigh's traditional chocolate Easter bunny. For more than 20 years, Haigh's has sold large and small bilbies in both milk and dark chocolate at Easter, with part-proceeds from every sale donated to RFA.

More recently, Haigh's has partnered with Zoos South Australia to raise awareness of the plight of the endangered bilby and is a major sponsor of the Adelaide Zoo's purpose-built bilby exhibit and its important breeding program. Haigh's has also partnered with government and community organisations in the Arid Recovery Project, which was established in 1997 to re-establish native wildlife and eradicate rabbits, foxes and feral cats from a 123 square kilometre reserve in northern South Australia.

Alister is a Fellow of the Australian Institute of Company Directors and a Life Member of Family Business Australia, having served on both the South Australian Committee and the

National Board. Simon is a board member of the Burnside War Memorial Hospital Foundation.

Reflections

Since its establishment in 1915, Haigh's has survived two World Wars, the Great Depression, unfavourable government regulations and the more recent Global Financial Crisis through a combination of good fortune, sound management and shrewd decisions over four generations.

There have been failures as well as successes, such as the Perth and Gold Coast stores, an attempt to boost sales by heavily promoting Valentine's Day and exporting to Japan, which turned out to be unsustainable without huge capital investment and mass production. Poorly performing shops have been closed or relocated. Commenting on these ventures, Simon argues:

> 'I don't class them as failures. I just don't class them as successes. They didn't work as well as planned and we learnt from them. When challenges arise we adapt.'

Throughout its history, Haigh's has been quick to admit and respond to setbacks and disappointments. 'None of them have been allowed to cause significant damage to the business,' says Simon. 'Nor have they prevented Haigh's from innovating and, on occasions, taking calculated risks.'

Haigh's Chocolates has set itself apart from most other confectionery manufacturers by resisting the temptation to increase volume because of a determination to maintain the quality of its products. Apart from a short-lived period of selling Easter eggs to supermarkets, John Haigh decided to sell his chocolates predominantly through its company-branded stores. Simon recalls his father saying to one supermarket chain after it demanded a price reduction, 'No, I don't need your contract. You've already paid for my machinery.' Simon points out, 'Most of our competitors and companies similar to us during John's era went down the wholesale path and most of them have now disappeared. Wholesalers are more exposed to defaulters or retailers that are slow to pay. We are successful because we control the supply chain the whole way through.'

> We are successful because we control the supply chain the whole way through.

From the very beginning back in 1915, the growth and success of Haigh's has been the result of a team effort, with significant contributions from within and outside the family. Lettie assisted Alfred in the making of sweets above the Beehive Corner shop and later went on to make cakes in the Haigh's Building until just after Alfred's death. Alfred's half-brother worked in the factory as a chocolate dipper. John Haigh's wife Mary had significant input into the Easter ranges after seeing the ranges of overseas confectioners while on trips abroad.

There have been numerous loyal employees who have remained with the company for all, most or a significant portion of their working life. Of particular note is Harold Lewis, who started working for Alfred Haigh in his Mount Gambier shop in 1911 at the age of 14, later following Alfred to Adelaide to work in the factory and in 1933 was appointed as factory manager, a position he held until his retirement in 1965 after 53 years with Haigh's.

Katy Schiavone started working for Haigh's in 1967 as a 14-year-old in the box room, folding, stapling and gluing cardboard to help create the distinctive Haigh's chocolate packaging. She also fulfilled several other roles, including adding decorations to chocolates and customer service at the factory door. More recently she has taken on the role of factory training officer and remains a loyal employee after 52 years with the company.

Alister Haigh is keen to acknowledge the role played by all team members, from executives to factory workers, shop managers and assistants, in the continuing success of Haigh's

Chocolates. Celebrating the company's centenary in 2015 he said:

> 'Simon and I are very fortunate to have worked with a great group of executives and team members who have made it possible for Haigh's to reach this centenary milestone.'

Haigh's Chocolates has only three directors, John, Alister and Simon, who directly own the shares they inherited from Alfred and Claude. The rest of the shares are held in two family trusts for other family members. 'We don't have formal board meetings because Dad doesn't believe in them,' says Simon. 'We are still able to have discussions around the kitchen or dining room table. If there is a difference of opinion, we talk about it. To his credit, Dad hasn't overturned any of our decisions, even if he hasn't agreed with them.' The directors don't make decisions in isolation. They have an executive team consisting of managers of marketing, finance, retailing, manufacturing and human relations to advise them on critical issues. Simon believes that the tightness of the shareholdings and governance is one of the biggest factors in the longevity and success of the business.

Simon, John and Alister Haigh with sacks of raw cocoa beans.

Moving forward

After decades of extensions to the Parkside factory, Haigh's opened a new multimillion-dollar cocoa bean processing factory in 2018, almost tripling the annual production of chocolate for Haigh's range of more than 250 products. Located in the Adelaide suburb of Mile End, it is now the largest cocoa bean processing plant in Australia and the most modern of its kind in the Southern Hemisphere. The additional production capacity will allow for continued growth in Australia and potentially overseas.

The flow of leadership from generation to generation has been smooth up until now. However, Simon contends, 'It won't surprise me if there is a period in the future when the business won't be run by a member of the family.' Alister Haigh is investigating succession planning through Family Business Australia (FBA). 'We're also working on setting up a family council and an advisory board, with guidance from FBA, which brings together the experience of other successful family businesses,' says Simon.

According to Simon, the business has outgrown the way it used to operate:

'Alister and I were jacks of all trades when we joined the business. We did bookwork and finance, we made the chocolate and did whatever we had to. Now it's much more specialised. The family will all be involved as owners but if members of the next generation want to work for the company, they will need to be the best qualified person to do the job. We'd like them to go out and learn – make their mistakes with other companies before they come back into the business. One of my regrets is that I didn't go and work for Cadbury, Mars or a similar company before joining the family business. It would have been beneficial but hindsight is a wonderful thing.'

The journey to perfection continues and it's fair to say that the destination keeps moving.

Knowledge is power

"Knowledge is power. Information is liberating. Education is the premise of progress, in every society, in every family."
Kofi Annan, seventh Secretary-General
of the United Nations, 23 June 1997

As Kofi Annan expressed so eloquently, the idiom 'knowledge is power' applies in every society and every family. It is also fundamental to the success of family businesses, which play such a crucial role in the Australian economy.

The eight family businesses featured in this book have accumulated a total of 1,109 years of knowledge. In this chapter, my aim is to unlock the cumulative knowledge of these successful family enterprises by identifying the characteristics and experiences that the businesses, despite their diversity, have in common.

It is not just an academic exercise. It's also an account of how resourceful people work together for a common goal over a long period of time, through generational transition and dramatic changes in society and technology.

The founders

The eight family businesses were all founded more than 100 years ago, when living conditions, educational opportunities and the whole social and cultural environment were very different to what they are today. Some of the founders travelled across the world to a country entirely different from their homeland. Others were brought to a new land by their parents. But they were all resourceful, ambitious and determined, and possessed unshakable self-belief and a relentless work ethic.

Those same characteristics are required by anyone planning to launch into a new business today. Establishing a business in the 21st century is, of course, very different but it would be wrong to say that it's easier. Today's pioneers have to be multi-skilled and capable of dealing with myriad regulations at federal, state and local government level – either that, or they need the capital behind them to pay for the required expertise.

The entrepreneurs

Without exception, all the founders featured in the book were entrepreneurs who were not averse to taking risks to develop their businesses. Lionel and William Samson opened their store in Fremantle to sell goods and livestock. The business quickly grew to become a liquor distributor, customs agent and auction house, largely due to Lionel's personality and entrepreneurial spirit. Although Thomas Cooper was able to create a unique ale, his business would not have flourished without his ability to sell it to private customers and gain the respect of affluent members of the community to allow him to borrow and build his business at substantial risk. Shortly after opening his Mount Gambier fruit and confectionery store, Alfred Haigh was operating fruit and refreshment stalls at local meetings and sporting events. Several years later, he was selling his products from a cart in the main street and had established a soft drink factory.

Entrepreneurship in the families has not been confined to the founders. For example, it was third-generation John Haigh who seized the initiative to take the confectionery business, established by his grandfather, to great heights in chocolate-making. It was second-generation John Charles Brown who opened a cellar door during the Great Depression, experimented with new grape varieties and inspired the next generation of Browns to follow his progressive path. The innovative Kindergarten Winery and acclaimed Epicurean Centre at Brown Brothers at Milawa, along with the company's expansion into Tasmania, can all be attributed to the legacy of John Charles. Fourth-generation Garry and Allyn Beard opened their first bedding store in China in 2013. Six years later, at the time of writing, there are more than 50 of their stores in China. For Coopers Brewery, entrepreneurship has manifested itself in breaking away from tradition, "getting out of the straitjacket", exemplified by the manufacture of DIY beer kits and expanding its range to include lagers and lighter beers.

Resilience and perseverance

The resilience and perseverance of successive generations of the eight families, and many others like them, is nothing short of astounding. They continued to trade through two World Wars while family members and employees left to serve their country in foreign lands. They all found ways to keep their businesses afloat and protect their employees from the worst effects of the Great Depression. In more recent times, they have adapted to massive changes in technology and continuing economic instability.

All enterprises depend on the land in one way or another. The family businesses profiled in this book are either totally dependent on agriculture, have interests in it, supply to farmers or rely on farm products for their raw materials. They have bounced back from the effects of droughts, floods, bushfires, hail and frost. Even the urban businesses have stared down fires that have destroyed their buildings or suffered losses due to floods.

Whole generations have withstood heartbreaking family tragedies that could have destroyed the will of many business owners to continue. The resilience of Thomas Cooper was remarkable. Having lost one daughter during infancy on the long voyage to

Australia in 1852, Thomas and his wife Ann suffered the loss of three more daughters during infancy in Adelaide. He remarried after Ann's tragic death at the age of 44, only to lose three infant sons from his second marriage. Through all of these tragedies, Thomas was also facing heavy debt. Yet, he continued to rebound from the setbacks and built the foundation for a business that has survived for more than 150 years.

Adapting to change

In order to survive for 100 years or more, a business must be able to adapt to changes in society, technology and the marketplace. When Lionel and William Samson landed at Fremantle in 1829, their goods and stock could only be brought in by ship and transported from the port by horse and cart. For almost 200 years, the Samson's business has evolved to adapt to massive changes such as the introduction of rail, motor vehicles and planes. As the first holder of a liquor licence in Western Australia, the business has seen a complete transformation of the beer and wine industry. The movement of goods across Australia has changed dramatically in response to new technology, sophisticated packaging and massive increases in population. Lionel Samson & Son could not have survived as auctioneers, merchants and shipping agents. The Lionel Samson Sadleirs Group now comprises rail and road transport services and packaging, along with the Plantagenet winery.

The Furphy family, still based in the regional Victorian city of Shepparton, manufactured agricultural machinery for farmers and city councils before and after the appearance of motor cars and tractors. By the 1980s, the demand for agricultural machinery and the size of the company's customer base were in serious decline, leading to the end of the production of the famous Furphy Farm Water Cart in 1983. The future was in engineering and galvanized steel and the foundry had to find new markets for cast iron products. As a family-owned business there was no easy solution, but ultimately it divided itself into two separate and quite distinctive companies with new products and different customer bases.

Over the generations, each of the family businesses has served up a mix of colourful characters, quiet achievers, men and women of faith, as well as the charismatic entrepreneurs. Some of them have been energetic agents of change who have redefined their family business, raised it to another level or saved it from self-destruction. Without these giants, these businesses could not have continued or enjoyed success for more than 100 years.

Second-generation Jack Samson masterminded the acquisition of Sadleirs by Samson & Son and arguably saved both businesses. Fourth-generation Maxwell Cooper had to battle older and conservative directors for years before being allowed to put his advanced training, experience and innovative ideas into practice. Fourth-generation Roger and Andrew Furphy made the agonising decision to split the business established by their great grandfather into two separate businesses in order to adapt to a vastly changing market. Third-generation John Pemberton Curlewis Forsyth sold his own business to buy out all other Dymocks shareholders, transformed the bookselling business into a modern enterprise and built a successful and diverse group of companies. Third-generation John Graham and Ross Brown continued to innovate as their father had done. Third-generation managing director Austin Beard worked on the factory floor with his men and developed an environment of mutual respect and loyalty that continues today. At Bulla Dairy, second-generation Jack Sloan, Bill Downey Senior and Keith Anderson oversaw the business through a period of unprecedented change in the dairy industry. Jack was managing director for a remarkable 44 years. Bill and Keith, although managing two plants separated by a distance of over 150 kilometres, spent hours on the phone each working day, keeping the depots working together seamlessly. Third-generation John Haigh believed that the future of the business established by his grandfather was in chocolate. He consequently travelled to Switzerland to learn about chocolate making from the best in the world and returned to take the Haigh's confectionery business to new heights.

Family values

There is an unmistakable pride within family enterprises that is difficult to replicate in other enterprises or organisations. There is much for all eight family businesses in this book to be proud of, though almost unanimously, they cite surviving more than 100 years as their greatest achievement.

When the family name is on the product, the label, the shopfront, the van or the truck, it is under scrutiny and it has to be backed up with a great product or service for success to follow in the marketplace. Ross Brown, retired executive director of the Brown Family Wine Group, contends that being labelled as a family business alone does not provide an advantage in the marketplace:

> 'It's not just about being a family business but having a brand that your customers or clients can relate to, backed up by family values.'

Family values are clearly visible in all of the successful businesses described in the pages of this book. They are transferred by example to employees and suppliers and contribute a great deal to the success and prosperity of the business, for mutual benefit. A common trait of the businesses is the unwavering loyalty and respect employees have for their employers and the business. I found numerous examples of several generations of the same family working for the business and employees happily admitting that they felt like they were part of the family.

Dr Tim Cooper suggests a reason for that loyalty:

'It's perhaps the custodial nature of the family ownership, where the family recognises the importance of the employees and their loyalty and are therefore attuned to rewarding that loyalty. In businesses like ours the importance of maintaining strong bonds with our employees is passed from one generation of the family to the next.'

In Steve Samson's submission to the 2012 Parliamentary Joint Committee Inquiry into Family Businesses in Australia he said:

'During the very tough times during the 1970s and '80s, when things were very, very tough, we made sure that we never sacked any person who was an employee of our business, because that is what the family wanted to do. They were willing to forgo a dividend, a profit, to make sure that we supported and protected those employees.'

Trust in and respect for family businesses is evident inside and outside the workplace. Both Coopers Brewery and A.H. Beard have been kept afloat by benefactors who had remarkable trust for individual family members. Thomas Cooper accumulated an overload of debt more than once and was still able to borrow from benefactors who respected his reputation for honesty and had faith in his product. When a competitor attempted to destroy A.H. Beard by taking advantage of its substantial debt in the late 1970s, the business was saved by a loan from a supplier because of its confidence in Austin Beard, his family business and his products. Again, in 2001, A.H. Beard was saved from debt, in this instance by a retailer with confidence in the future of the family and its products.

Bulla family values

Bulla Dairy articulates the family values it shares with its employees, customers and suppliers.

BULLA FAMILY VALUES

Our family values underpin our success as a business, they are the beliefs and ethics that determine how we behave as individuals and as a company.

We are a family

The Bulla family is unified and supportive. We value strong relationships, cherish our traditions and celebrate our successes. Building mutual trust is fundamental to our family's success.

Achieving our goals together

We work together to achieve our goals with a spirit of cooperation. We are honest about the challenges we face and resolve issues together.

Courage to think differently

We challenge the way things are done today, to improve continually and achieve our potential.

Hear and be heard

We respect, consider and value each other's ideas and perspective.

Customer at heart

Customers, both internal and external, are central to our thinking and decision making. We focus on satisfying the needs of all our customers.

Leadership by all

We are leaders within our business. Leaders are visible, approachable, seize opportunities and welcome responsibility.

Family values, however expressed, are critical to the success and longevity of family businesses.

The changing role of women

All of the businesses explored in this book were dominated by males until the 21st century, with some notable exceptions. When an incumbent retired it was a son who took his place. It was almost always the sons who inherited the business upon the death of the head of the previous generation. The daughters were left with property and cash.

Yet, in some cases, women have been among the giants of the businesses, often unacknowledged for their contributions. When Lionel Samson brought his young wife Fanny to the colony of Western Australia she was still in her late teens. But she got on with life and maintained a strong presence in the business even after her husband's death. Their daughter-in-law Katharine had a much stronger influence on the business. When her husband William died at a young age she became the sole owner. She kept a tight rein and watchful eye on the business while it was operated on a day-to-day basis by external managers until her death at the age of 95. John Charles Brown and his wife Patricia worked as a team. Patricia was included in the decision-making process in the business and, by reputation, had the last word on many occasions. While Ada Beard helped her husband Albert make mattress covers, she also kept a very close eye on the business and managed all expenditure 'with an iron fist'. According to her grandson Allyn, the business would not have survived without her.

Women are increasingly represented in senior management and on boards. Gender is no longer a factor in appointment or recruitment. Five of the eight families have at least one female director sitting on their board. In acknowledgement of a female member of the family being appointed to its board, the business Cooper & Sons changed its name to Coopers Brewery Ltd. The Brown Family Wine Group's fourth generation is dominated by women, with Eliza Brown on the board and Katherine Brown as the first female winemaker in the family. Katherine's sisters,

Caroline and Emma, work in the business. Eliza's sister Angela also works in the wine industry. The change of the company name from Brown Brothers to the Brown Family Wine Group is an acknowledgement of women's participation in the business at all levels, as well as a response to the acquisition of other vineyards, wineries and brands in Tasmania and Victoria.

Long-term vision and succession planning

There is strong agreement within the families that they have a long-term vision, which is in contrast to corporations who have to respond more quickly to shareholders in the event of a setback. They agree that family businesses are more patient. They also constantly reinvesting in the business to secure a profitable future.

Several submissions and witness statements to the 2012 Parliamentary Joint Committee Inquiry emphasised the long-term mindset of family businesses. Professor Ken Moores, executive chairman of Moores Family Enterprise and founding director of Bond University's Australian Centre for Family Business, told the committee:

> 'The long-term mindset of family businesses provides resilience in times of economic downturn, greater retention of labour and an effort to preserve their communities around them.'

He added:

> 'The average CEO of a family business is there for about 20 years. The average CEO of a non-family firm is there for about 3.89 years and going down. If you think about that for a moment, this is a person who has been there, learnt their job and has got the time and capacity to pass it on to the next generation, because they have learned a bit of wisdom.'

Professor Moore talks about 'wisdom'. There is much more to wisdom than knowledge. Each of the families featured in this book has passed on characteristics such as persistence, resilience and entrepreneurship. In my view, family businesses are able to sustain these traits for much longer periods than other enterprises. In a family business, the next generation is exposed to role models who teach by example. The families talk about the business to each other around the kitchen table. Sons and daughters have grown up in the business environment, some even getting up to mischief in the office. Sometimes they are even inspired by watching and listening to workers on the factory floor. They've seen the hard work, the passion and the rewards. Some, like the Furphys and the Beards, have seen the pain associated with dramatic restructure of the business that is necessarily entangled with family relationships. They've seen how apparent setbacks often provide opportunities and how to respond when errors are made.

A key theme of the 2012 Parliamentary Inquiry report is the need for a clear succession plan. While each family has its own unique approach to succession planning, there are some common threads. All strongly believe that:

- being a member of the family is not a free ticket to employment in leadership roles in the family business – employment or promotion must be based on merit

- there should be no pressure on family members to join the company or become directors

- it is beneficial for the next generation to work elsewhere before joining the family business.

There is also consensus that a succession plan cannot be set in concrete. It must be reviewed regularly. Ross Brown of the Brown Family Wine Group says, 'The process of succession planning is never finished. You can't just lock it away. It's a continuous journey.' Each family and each generational transition is different. There is no "one rule fits all". An effective succession plan must be a living, breathing document that accounts for differences between generations along with a largely unpredictable diversity of ambitions and personalities. It must take into account the inevitable tension between tradition and acceptance of change.

One common element in successful generational transfer is the ability of the older generation to step back and give their successors the opportunity to learn the skills of leadership at an early age, sometimes by making mistakes along the way. Adam Furphy had no experience in the family business apart from casual work as a youngster during the school holidays when his father Andrew retired in 1998. As Andrew's only son and a natural successor, he was quickly launched into a position of leadership. The transition worked because there were loyal and long-standing employees on the floor who made his job easier. Adam credits his father's ability to step back for the successful transition. 'He had a knack for picking the right person for each job and let them get on with it,' says Adam. Dymocks Chairman, John Forsyth, makes the same point:

> 'This business was my dream not my children's. They have different dreams. My job is to make sure that I have the best managing directors in each of our businesses so there can be a seamless transfer when I go. I have to let the managing directors make mistakes. I can't breathe down their neck. They need to be able to do things their way. That's one of the most important things for a family-owned group. Extremely competent executives, appointed on merit and with the right skill set, are vital. If you micro-manage them and you drop dead, it tends to fall apart.'

Even when there is no apparent heir, as was the case when William Fredrick Samson passed away in 1900 at the age of only 44 with no will and three children aged 18, 17 and 14, the business continued into the next generation. His widow, Katharine Samson remained in the background while a succession of managers from outside the family successfully led the business for more than 30 years until William's younger son Jack, then his sons and his daughter's sons, took day-to-day management of the business back into family hands.

With support available from organisations like Family Business Australia (FBA), KPMG, the Family Business Education and Research Group (FBERG) at the University of Adelaide and the Australian Small Business and Family Enterprise Ombudsman among others, family businesses are in a much stronger position to prepare for generational transfer than ever before. Two of the businesses, the Lionel Samson Sadleirs Group and A.H. Beard, with the support of FBA, have set up family councils, which provide a conduit between shareholders and the board. This additional line of communication facilitates productive discussion and decision making about issues such as family engagement and succession. Haigh's Chocolates is currently in the process of setting up a family council and advisory board with guidance from FBA.

Governance

All families featured in *Family Business Success Stories*, with one exception, are governed by a board of directors. The exception is the Furphy family, where Adam Furphy is sole director of J. Furphy & Son and Sam Furphy is sole director of Furphy Foundry. Each of them works with an effective management team. 'Family businesses like ours are made up of many people making different contributions,' says Adam. Sam and Adam both have faith in senior management teams and employees, just as their predecessors had. 'A capable, engaged and accountable management team that is given the right mix of autonomy and direction can be a very effective structure for the success and longevity of a family-owned business,' says Adam. His cousin Sam agrees.

Of the seven boards of the other families, five include directors who are not members of the family. All eight businesses recognise that if family members with the required qualifications and experience to sit on the board are not available, positions must be filled by independent directors. The businesses have all grown immensely and the environment in which they operate is much more sophisticated than when they were founded. Even when governance at board level is exclusively in family hands, they draw on the wealth of knowledge and experience in their senior management teams.

As family shareholders grew in number through the generations, or became more distant, some of the businesses arrived at a point that could have rendered them unmanageable or unprofitable. There is no future in a family business with too many people with conflicting ambitions pulling in different directions. This has occurred in the past within four of the eight family businesses, precipitating in a restructure or buyout that has prevented their collapse.

In 1936, Harry Sadleir and Jack Samson presided over the acquisition of 90% of shares of R.C. Sadleir by Lionel Samson & Son when the former was in danger of stagnation or collapse. Today, the Sadleirs transport and infrastructure enterprises dominate the Lionel Samson Sadleirs Group. In 1960, to ensure the continuation of J. Furphy & Sons, third-generation Jack Furphy acquired the shares of his two cousins because they had no male heirs; Jack had four sons. Twenty-nine years later, Jack's sons Roger and Andrew split the business into two for the benefit of future generations.

John Pemberton Curlewis Forsyth's acquisition of all other Dymocks' shareholders in 1981 kept the business in family hands when it was treading water and had an uncertain future. And when two of his sisters and his mother were intent on selling the family business, third-generation Austin Beard put his home and personal possessions on the line to buy them out to save it for future generations.

Giving back

All eight family businesses have been firmly engaged with the communities in which they operate and the broader business community since their establishment. They are all committed to giving back in one way or another. Most have been involved in state or local government and a wide variety of community organisations and industry bodies, including the Australian Institute of Company Directors and FBA. Family members from these businesses have been elected to local councils, served as mayors or been recognised with medals of the Order of Australia for philanthropy or contributions to their communities or respective industries.

They all give back to the broader Australian and international communities with a commitment to environmental sustainability. Some have gone to extraordinary lengths to conserve water and energy, often with benefits to their bottom line as well as the environment. One example that stands out is Coopers Brewery's huge investment in its own onsite power and desalination plants. All companies embrace recycling in a variety of ways. Successful family businesses recognise that the sustainability of their business depends on the sustainability of the environment, the communities on which they impact and the welfare of their employees. Climate change is a common concern – without a healthy planet the business goes nowhere.

All of the family businesses support charitable organisations and some have established their own charitable foundations or formally partnered with other philanthropic organisations. Of particular note are the Coopers Brewery Foundation and the Dymocks Literary Foundation.

Looking forward

Looking to the future, none of the families have any intention of selling their businesses established so many years ago. Sam Furphy, when asked about selling, says:

> 'I believe in giving my children the same opportunity that I and the previous generations have enjoyed. It would be hard to deny them that.'

Garry Beard says, 'We enjoy what we do and we have an obligation to our team, customers and suppliers.' A.H. Beard has a rule in its shareholders agreement that requires 'a 100% unanimous vote' to sell the business. 'That's very unlikely,' he says.

Steve Samson comments on the broader picture of the future of family businesses:

> 'We employ over half of Australia's workforce and the government didn't really appreciate the importance of the family business sector. It was through FBA's participation in the Parliamentary Joint Senate Inquiry into Family Businesses in Australia that it realised the extent of the sector and the need for more government understanding.'

The 2012 Inquiry led to the establishment of the office of the Australian Small Business and Family Enterprise Ombudsman (ASBFEO) in March 2016 and the appointment of Kate Carnell as ombudsman. The legislation that established the ASBFEO was the first significant recognition by the Australian government of the importance of family businesses, all of which begin as small businesses. When the Hon Bruce Billson, Minister for Small Business, announced the legislation he said:

> 'This is the very first time in our nation's history that the words "family enterprise" are used in the title of legislation. Ensuring "family enterprise" is recognised in this legislation

reflects the high respect the government holds for the hard-working women and men who make up our small business community.'

Reflecting on the journeys

The journeys undertaken by each of the eight families have been far from smooth. There have been family tragedies, unpredictable setbacks and errors of judgement along the way, including quite a few examples of inappropriate acquisitions and diversification. On the other hand, there have been financial rewards and an immense sense of satisfaction and achievement.

The stories about these families and their enterprise send a strong message to Australian consumers about the social, cultural and economic value of family-owned businesses. They also provide valuable insights into entrepreneurship, resilience and the challenge of planning and managing the interaction between family members and the business.

THE UNIVERSITY
of ADELAIDE

For over 140 years, we've pushed the boundaries in business education, delivering innovative and transformative courses and producing a network of alumni who have gone on to make a real-world impact in the world of business.

With an enviable roster of teaching staff and global partners, the Adelaide Business School provides a range of cutting-edge teaching and research options. Our programs produce business leaders across a range of disciplines, including Accounting, Finance, Marketing, Management, International Management, Entrepreneurship, Project Management and our top-ranked MBA.

The Adelaide Business School is proud to support the millions of family business owners across Australia – we are home to the Family Business Education and Research Group whose work has furthered family enterprises across Australia, and the world.

In recognition that innovation is an integral part of modern business, the Entrepreneurship, Innovation and Commercialisation Centre (ECIC) forms part of the Adelaide Business School. As such, we continue to operate the longest running and most successful pre-accelerator program in Australia (eChallenge) and the global network of ThincLab Incubators established in 1993.

Just as our students and academics benefit from our strong industry partnerships, organisations also gain access to a range of business opportunities by working with us to meet your company's strategic goals.

A Business School partnership enables our partners to benefit widely on a variety of fronts including:

- building brand awareness, relevance and relationships through targeted interaction with Business School faculty, students and alumni

- framing business practices and policy through research

- engaging with students by sponsoring scholarships and industry prizes

- priority intern and graduate recruitment support

- networking and benchmarking with local and international service industry professionals and experts

- contributing to the strategic orientation of the School.

If you are interested in getting involved with the Adelaide Business School, please contact us for more information on how to get started.

www.business.adelaide.edu.au

**Family Business
Australia**

At Family Business Australia (FBA) our purpose is to help family businesses succeed.

We do this by assisting family businesses to harness their unique competitive advantage. Leveraging 'family business' as an asset is what truly sets our members apart from their competition and FBA has been successfully helping family businesses along that path for the past 20 years!

- Family run businesses account for 70% of all businesses in Australia

- More than 60% of trading businesses in Australia are family businesses

- There are more than 1.4 million Australian family businesses operating in Australia

- Australians prefer to buy from family businesses.

At FBA, we tailor solutions to family business members through facilitating and engaging resources and channels that promote success and foster sustainability. Our programs and products are developed to build stronger families and healthier businesses.

There's a certain understanding and trust that comes when working with a family business. When family members work together, and share their wins and achievements, it's not just a job – they have the future of their family invested. This is often reflected in their business practices and how they relate to their clients and customers, who benefit from that investment and trust.

Membership with FBA ensures you are immersed in the family business community. We work in the space where family, business and ownership all intersect. Our education programs and special events are designed to generate opportunities for families in business to learn and grow, by networking and sharing with their peers. We provide access to specialist family, business and technical services.

What we do

We provide access to education and training for family-specific and general business development, and generate opportunities for families in business to learn and grow by networking and sharing with their peers.

Professional Development: FBA holds a range of courses and programs over the calendar year to assist family business individuals, their advisers, directors and employees to create a sustainable and professional family business. Course presenters and facilitators selected have had significant work and academic experience in the field of family business, providing participants access to deep understanding and practical lessons that can be taken back to their own business.

Professional Peer Forums: The FBA Forum Program is the only professionally facilitated, executive discussion group for family business leaders, executives and CEOs in Australia. Forum groups are made up of 10 family business leaders, meeting 10 times per year.

Family Business Advisers: Are you looking for family business help, support and advice? FBA has a network of Accredited Advisers who can help you reach your family business goals, build a body of knowledge and guide your family to work together more effectively.

Family Business Network: Our community is made up of family business leaders, the next generation, family members and independent directors and advisers from a multitude of different businesses from all industries. FBA provides the opportunity to connect with this network, share knowledge and stories and better understand what it takes to be a successful family business.

Events: The FBA calendar is packed with events throughout Australia including Family Business Insiders, National Conference, State Family Business Insights, Workshops, Webinars and more.

Find out more at **www.familybusiness.org.au**

Sources and further reading

General

Australian Bureau of Statistics, http://abs.gov.au

Australian Small Business and Family Enterprise Ombudsman, https://www.asbfeo.gov.au

Family Business Australia, https://www.familybusiness.org.au

Gibson, Candy (2006) 'Families get down to business', *Adelaidean*, University of Adelaide, https://www.adelaide.edu.au/adelaidean/ issues/16521/news16611.html

KPMG Enterprise, Family Business Australia and the University of Adelaide's Family Business Education and Research Group (2018) *Family business – the balance for success*, The 2018 KPMG Enterprise and Family Business Australia survey report, KPMG https://assets.kpmg/content/dam/kpmg/au/pdf/2018/family-business-survey-2018-report.pdf

Parliamentary Joint Committee on Corporations and Financial Services (2013) *Family Businesses in Australia – different and significant: why they shouldn't be overlooked*, Commonwealth of Australia

RMIT and MGI Australasia (2013) *Surviving, Not Thriving: The MGI Australian Family and Private Business Survey 2013* (Executive Summary), MGI Australasia, https://www.asbfeo.gov. au/sites/default/files/MGI-FB-Survey-2013.pdf

Chapter 1

Fremantle Shipping News (2017) *Interview with Bill Samson*, https://fremantleshippingnews.com.au/2017/02/27/ interview-with-bill-samson/

Gillard, Garry (2016) *Samson Family*, https://fremantlestuff.info/ people/samson.html

Goulder, Sandra and Cooper, Bill (1995) *Out of the West: The Story of Sadliers Transport 1895-1995*, Sadliers Transport

Hitchcock, J. K. (1929) *The History of Fremantle: The Front Gate of Australia*, 1829-1929, at Fremantle Stuff, https://fremantlestuff.info/hitchcock.html

Lambert, Desmond A. (2004) *The Lionel Samson Story: A brief history of Australia's oldest family business*, Lionel Samson and Son

Levi, John S. et al. (1974) *Australian genesis: Jewish convicts and settlers*, 1788-1850, Rigby

Moore, George Fletcher (2018) *Diary of Ten Years Eventful Life of an Early Settler in Western Australia*, Franklin Classics Trade Press (First published in 1884)

National Trust of Western Australia, www.nationaltrust.org.au/wa

Parliament of Western Australia, http://www.parliament.wa.gov.au

Smith, Sean (2017) 'Oldest WA firm has a road map to rebuild its brands', *The West Australian*, https://thewest.com.au/business/oldest-wa-firm-has-a-road-map-to-rebuild-its-brands-ng-b88504490z

White, Louis (2014) 'Keeping it in the family', *Sydney Morning Herald*, https://www.smh.com.au/business/small-business/keeping-it-in-the-family-20140717-3c2xu.html

Chapter 2

Coopers Brewery Ltd (2013) 'Recycling saves money for Coopers, raises it for charity', *Sustainability Matters*, https://www.sustainabilitymatters.net.au/content/waste/article/recycling-saves-money-for-coopers-raises-it-for-charity-709296718

Painter, Alison, Cooper, Tim and Linn, Rob (2013) *Jolly Good Ale and Old: Coopers Brewery 1862-2012*, 3rd Edition, Coopers Brewery Ltd

Stubbs, Dr Brett J. (2012) 'Beer and war in Australia', *Brews News*, https://www.brewsnews.com.au/2012/07/17/beer-and-war-in-australia/

Chapter 3

Barnes, John (1998) *Made in Shepparton: The history of J. Furphy & Sons 1873-1998*, J. Furphy & Sons

Barnes, John and Furphy, Andrew (2005) *Furphy: The Water Cart and The Word*, Australian Scholarly Publishing

Furphy, Roger (1996) *Two Brothers: A Bit of a Yarn*, Primavera Press
Lexico, www.lexico.com
Victorian Places: Shepparton, http://www.victorianplaces.com.au/
   shepparton

Chapter 4

The Dymocks Building, *About the Dymocks Building*,
   https://www.thedymocksbuilding.com.au/about-dymocks
New South Wales Office of Environment & Heritage,
   https://www.environment.nsw.gov.au
State Heritage Inventory, *Commercial Building "Dymocks" Including
   Interiors*, NSW Government Office of Environment & Heritage,
   https://www.environment.nsw.gov.au/heritageapp/
   ViewHeritageItemDetails.aspx?ID=2424010
Sydney Architecture, http://sydneyarchitecture.com
Tyrrell, James R (1952) *Old Books, Old Friends*, Old Sydney, Angus
   and Robertson

Chapter 5

Dunstan, Keith (1999) *Not a bad drop: Brown Brothers*, Utber &
   Patullo Publishing
Hudson, Sarah (2019) 'Brown Brothers wine: Katherine Brown on
   joining the family business', *The Weekly Times*, 1 May 2019.
   Accessed online at https://www.weeklytimesnow.com.au
Lofts, Graeme (2010) *Heart & Soul: Australia's First Families of Wine*,
   John Wiley & Sons Australia

Chapter 6

A.H. Beard (2015) 'A.H. Beard Puts Family First', *Business Chief*,
   1 July 2015, https://anz.businesschief.com/AH-Beard/profiles/
   170/AH-Beard-Puts-Family-First
Beard, Garry (2017) *A.H. Beard – Industry Leader S04*,
   https://youtu.be/b4DQl7yR-5Y
Whitcomb, Dorothy (2016) 'A.H. Beard Pty. Ltd. Thrives on Family
   Tradition', *BedTimes*, 2 June 2016, https://bedtimesmagazine.
   com/2016/06/h-beard-pty-ltd-thrives-family-tradition/

Chapter 7

AFN staff writers (2013) 'Bulla buys "choc top" ice cream company', *Australian Food News*, 8 July 2013, http://www.ausfoodnews.com.au/2013/07/08/bulla-buys-%E2%80%98choc-top%E2%80%99-ice-cream-company.html

Australian food history timeline, https://australianfoodtimeline.com.au

Barnes, Scott (2013) 'Factory's multi-million dollar boost', *Colac Herald*, 8 March 2013, https://colacherald.com.au/2013/03/44028/

Donati, Laura (2010) *Bulla – 100 Years of Real Dairy Goodness*, Regal Cream Pty Ltd

Kohler, Alan (2014) 'A dairy gold mine that's not for sale', *Family Business Magazine*, December 2014

Martin, Alison (2014) '$7M cream separator begins at Colac plant', *Colac Herald*, 5 November 2014, https://colacherald.com.au/2014/11/7m-cream-separator-begins-colac-plant/

Chapter 8

Australian War Memorial, 'United States forces in Australia', https://www.awm.gov.au/articles/encyclopedia/homefront/us_forces

City of Adelaide, https://www.cityofadelaide.com.au

Ergo, 'Food shortages & rationing', State Library of Victoria, http://ergo.slv.vic.gov.au/explore-history/australia-wwii/home-wii/food-shortages-rationing

Santich, Barbara (2015) *Haigh's Chocolates: Enjoyed for Generations*, Wakefield Press

Chapter 9

United Nations Secretary-General (1997) '"If information and knowledge are central to democracy, they are conditions for development", says Secretary-General', *United Nations Press Release SG/SM/6268*, 23 June 1997, https://www.un.org/press/en/1997/19970623.sgsm6268.html

Index

CPSIA information can be obtained
at www.ICGtesting.com
Printed in the USA
BVHW070823190819
556214BV00003B/190/P